PETER PENNOYER ARCHITECTS

PETER PENNOYER ARCHITECTS

APARTMENTS ❦ TOWNHOUSES ❦ COUNTRY HOUSES

Anne Walker

FOREWORD BY ROBERT A. M. STERN

THE VENDOME PRESS
NEW YORK

CONTENTS

FOREWORD BY ROBERT A. M. STERN | 16
INTRODUCTION | 20

APARTMENTS
29

Fifth Avenue Triplex 30

East Side Duplex 38

Park Avenue Apartment 46

East River Apartment 54

TOWNHOUSES
63

Carnegie Hill Brownstone 64

Beaux-Arts Townhouse 72

Lenox Hill Townhouse 80

Limestone Mansion 90

Upper East Side Townhouse 100

Grosvenor Atterbury Townhouse 108

San Francisco House 118

COUNTRY HOUSES
127

Adirondack Camp 128

House on Penobscot Bay 136

Diamond A Ranch 146

House in the Santa Lucia Range 156

Meadow Lane House 164

Oakley Farm 170

Federal House 180

Beach House 190

Drumlin Hall 196

PROJECTS | 208
PHOTO AND DRAWING CREDITS | 222
ACKNOWLEDGMENTS | 223

FOREWORD
BY ROBERT A. M. STERN

OPPOSITE

In the Grosvenor Atterbury Townhouse, PPA transformed a formerly low and broad opening between the music room and dining room with a cross vault framed by paired pilasters.

OVERLEAF

The parlor level of the Carnegie Hill Brownstone, organized around an arched enfilade, revels in a playful layering of architectural details revealing the height and depth of the space.

Peter Pennoyer is one of the leading lights among today's Modern Traditional architects. Well established as one of our leading historians of twentieth-century traditional architecture—he documents for our benefit the work of significant but hitherto neglected architects such as Delano & Aldrich, Grosvenor Atterbury, and Warren & Wetmore in scholarly monographs co-written with Anne Walker, and no doubt advised by Gregory Gilmartin, his director of design, who is likewise a formidable historian—Pennoyer is also, as this book makes abundantly clear, a gifted designer with a wide range of stunning projects to his firm's credit. Taken together, his work as historian and architect enriches the discourse by bringing us one step closer to the lost history of twentieth-century traditional architecture. His career exemplifies an ideal too little valued: the architect as public intellectual. Bravo to him for that!

Pennoyer's investigations into the past are more than mere intellectual exercises: they are the fuel that feeds his creativity in the present. Pennoyer's scholarly and unironic stance not only places him above the fray but also transcends pettiness to embrace a discourse about architecture as both an art of social responsibility and cultural expression. I applaud the mix of scholarship and invention that undergirds all of Pennoyer's work.

When faced with the challenge of adding new to old, a very modern type of challenge, he does not disappoint. Pennoyer's capacity to bring back to life forlorn relics, like the neglected apartment interiors and townhouses that abound in this book, is second to none. Where most designers undertaking such work seek to impose their own signature, Pennoyer, digging deep into the original, restores or where necessary invents anew. His handling of stairs, vaulted ceilings, and molding profiles is always appropriate and always fresh.

Freshness of approach and a delightfully light hand are equally apparent in his designs for new houses, which exhibit a wide-ranging command of local vernacular styles, whether in the Adirondack woods or the coast of Maine or the parched landscape of New Mexico. Even in the overachieving precincts of Dutchess County, pomposity is avoided.

The Modern Traditionalism that Pennoyer's work so convincingly advances at first glance seems about as far from "cutting edge" as one can get. But is it? I'd say no. In the context of our time, it is radical, taking its place in a discourse that breaks with

the relentless present-ism of stylistic modernism that has monopolized contemporary architecture since the Second World War. Modern Traditional work looks back in order to go forward. It seeks to add on to the culture, not to disrupt it. Modern Traditionalism embodies the "historical sense" that T. S. Eliot celebrated: that "sense of the timeless as well as of the temporal," that sense that makes writers, or in this case architects, "acutely conscious of…[their] place in time, of…[their] contemporaneity."[1]

I first encountered Peter Pennoyer when, as an undergraduate at Columbia, he was my student. He was then, as he is now, a delight to know—a person to learn from even as one has the senior role of teacher. Pennoyer went on to Columbia's graduate professional program and was again my student. I felt twice blessed—thrice so after he interned in my professional office. At Columbia, Pennoyer was not alone as a "revolutionary" student; Gregory Gilmartin, with whom I was to collaborate on two books, and Tom Nugent are both now part of Pennoyer's atelier. There were others as well, like Roger Seifter and Randy Correll, now partners of mine, and Thomas Kligerman, John Ike, and Oscar Shamamian, also students at Columbia and later interns in my office who have gone on to successful independent practice specializing in traditional work.

The architects of the first Post-Modern generation took it on the chin for challenging the Modernist hegemony. Now the "younger" generation of (Post-) Modern Traditionalists is to be celebrated for staying the course. Pennoyer and his generation have everything to be proud of as they have grown into their maturity. As the work in this volume makes abundantly clear, among them Peter Pennoyer is a leader—a talent with a brain. With every project and book he has rightfully earned an important place in the architectural history of the twenty-first century.

---

[1] T. S. Eliot, "Tradition and the Individual Talent," in *The Secret Wood: Essays on Poetry and Criticism* (London: Methuen, 1920), 49.

INTRODUCTION

ABOVE
A poolhouse in Greenwich, Connecticut, is distinguished by a classical portico, columns, and bull's-eye window.

OPPOSITE
The cedar-shingled House in the Santa Lucia Range reflects the Pacific Coast Arts and Crafts tradition and will weather to embrace its natural surroundings.

THE WORK OF PETER PENNOYER ARCHITECTS IS AN INSPIRED convergence of scholarship and creativity. The twenty projects featured in this volume—ranging from apartment renovations set within the confines of Manhattan's street grid to new houses in the unimpeded wilds of the Pacific coast—represent the continuum of classical language, imaginatively reinterpreted, which succeed in throwing off the negative associations sometimes suggested by the labels "classical" or "traditional." While the firm has built a substantial and varied body of work, Peter Pennoyer maintains, "everything about architecture resides in the concept of the house." Ultimately, each project stands as a collaborative effort that synthesizes the premises of the commission, the voice of the client, and the creative talents of the architects, designers, craftsmen, and artists.

As chairman of the Institute of Classical Architecture & Classical America, Pennoyer is a leader in advocating the relevance of history and the classical idiom to current practice. But as devoted a traditionalist as he is today, Pennoyer and his partners did not arrive at this position predictably. Indeed, the arc of Pennoyer's career grew out of the contentious argument that unfolded between the Grays and the Whites, two self-appointed camps of architects who drew battle lines between modernism and postmodernism in the late 1970s. As a rejection of the formal functionalism of the modern aesthetic, postmodernism flourished as an effort to bring soul and meaning back into architecture through context, allusion, and ornament.

Born and raised in New York City, Pennoyer grew up enveloped by the classically inspired buildings, apartments, and townhouses of a landscape primarily shaped by Beaux-Arts–trained architects. As he was absorbing the qualities of his surroundings, Pennoyer's curiosity was piqued by his father's involvement in the New York City Art Commission (now called the Public Design Commission), a body responsible for overseeing all construction, renovation, and restoration of art, architecture, and landscape design on public land; this interest was later translated into high school internships at the New York Landmarks Preservation Commission and the Planning Commission. At Columbia University, Pennoyer found his mentor in the charismatic and inspiring Robert A. M. Stern, under whom he studied as both an undergraduate and a graduate student. Pennoyer recalled one long M4 bus ride up to 116th Street and Broadway, when Stern urged him to join his design studio and to stop frittering away his undergraduate years as a French literature major. Those who know Stern know he can be persuasive and Pennoyer followed the suggestion. Rife with polemics, Columbia in the late 1970s and early 1980s was a challenging place for the nascent historicist. While students learned about—and in Pennoyer's case delighted in—architectural history, they were also taught to feel an almost puritanical revulsion at the idea that historical styles could apply to current practice. During this time, "some architects," Marcus Whiffen of *American Architecture Since 1780* described, "went so far as to regard the historians as necrophilous disturbers of the graveyards of the past, who might at any moment disinter a corpse whose style was still capable of infecting the living." The instruction of the tenets of classical architecture, as it applied to design, fell through the cracks and Pennoyer and some of his classmates were chastised, in the words of one professor, for "sleepwalking through history." And while postmodernism revealed chinks in modernist dogma and reopened the dialogue between design and the influences of the past—a window that had been vehemently shut by the modernists since the Depression— its ironic stance and exaggerated references left Pennoyer and some of his more classically inclined colleagues seeking more.

During school, Pennoyer worked as a designer in Stern's office, which was then a small and young practice comprised primarily of Columbia students and recent graduates. Within an invigorating, collegial, and often challenging environment—something of a modern-day version of the Beaux-Arts atelier—Pennoyer and his colleagues, though relatively inexperienced, were driven on by Stern to tackle large and complex projects. It was a matter of being in the right place at the right time. Stern gave Pennoyer not only direction and focus but also an education.

In 1984 Pennoyer, in partnership with classmate Peter Moore, took on his first independent commission: a duplex loft in TriBeCa's American Thread Building for actress Isabella Rossellini. With Moore, who had been decorating apartments and lofts independently since his high school days, Pennoyer embarked on a series of small apartment renovations—or "miracle makeovers" as they called them—for models, artists, and figures in the fashion world. They had fun with architecture, experimenting with modern styles and taking on a range of colorful clients. In the Greenwich Village loft of fashion designer Zoran, Pennoyer designed an all-white, ultra-minimalist space with resin flooring and a basic shower—really just a showerhead and drain—in the open living area. The celebrated Pop Shop on Lafayette Street for the late artist and eighties icon Keith Haring incorporated undulating walls covered with Haring's bold and distinctive graffiti; commissions for Haring's loft studio on lower Broadway and renovations to Andy Warhol's Factory followed.

While other projects from the early 1980s (done in partnership with James Turino) reflected postmodern influences, the exaggerated way of manipulating form and applying ornament to convey historical meaning evolved into a more mature and nuanced classical aesthetic. Joined by former Columbia classmates Thomas P. R. Nugent and Gregory Gilmartin (a coauthor with Stern of the comprehensive *New York 1900* and *New York 1930*

BELOW

The design of Keith Haring's Pop Shop, completed in 1986, incorporated undulating walls and the artist's bold graffiti.

and author of *Shaping the City: New York and the Municipal Art Society*), the practice began to gravitate away from the use of self-conscious forms toward a more graceful and engaged approach that absorbed and elegantly distilled the qualities of context. In the Mark Hotel—a project completed under the aegis Pennoyer Turino Architects—Pennoyer and his partners embraced the tact, appropriateness, and fluid classicism for which he has come to be known. This commission, a transformation of a Madison Avenue apartment hotel with elegant Georgian interiors, embodied the firm's ability to simultaneously preserve the integrity and spirit of the original building while reinventing and enhancing it to embrace modern standards. The Mark reopened to much fanfare in 1990, the same year that Peter Pennoyer Architects was established.

This delicate balance of modern and historic and the ability to make the act of design seem natural has earned PPA the opportunity to work on many architecturally significant houses within many of New York's historic districts. While most of the firm's city projects are located in areas protected by the Landmarks Preservation Commission, the Blumka Gallery and house, completed in 1996, fell just outside the reach of the Upper East Side Historic District and provided the chance to design a new facade—a rare opportunity in New York. Here PPA transformed a stripped Italianate row house into a sequence of gallery and living spaces set behind a classically composed limestone-plaster facade. Meanwhile, the careful restoration of the Colony Club's Georgian ballroom and various projects at the Knickerbocker Club, including the design of a rooftop terrace restaurant, sparked Pennoyer's interest in the underdocumented work of Delano & Aldrich, an early-twentieth-century firm buoyed by its fresh and distilled reading of traditional sources. At the Knickerbocker Club, Pennoyer found a trove of the firm's original drawings, a discovery that inspired a monograph on William Adams Delano and his partner Chester Aldrich and their uniquely American conservative classical approach. The desire to unearth the work of other important early-twentieth-century architects obscured from collective memory by the onslaught of the International Style led Pennoyer to coauthor additional books, including *The Architecture of Warren & Wetmore* and *The Architecture of Grosvenor Atterbury*. PPA would later translate its scholarship into the LEED-gold-certified design for the Hotchkiss School's Paul Nitze Center for Global

ABOVE

Formerly a stripped rowhouse, a classical limestone facade transformed the Blumka Galley and house.

BELOW

An elegant enfilade of rooms in the Paul Nitze Center for Global Understanding and Independent Thinking at the Hotchkiss School, formerly the Monahan Gymnasium, captures the spirit of Delano & Aldrich's conservative classical approach.

ABOVE

A double-height top-lit library anchors the interior of the Auchincloss house, reflecting the firm's capacity to sculpt space.

ABOVE RIGHT

The Auchincloss's Catskills retreat was inspired by Gunnar Asplund's Villa Snellman and refined with classical details.

Understanding and Independent Thinking, an enfilade of rooms carved out of the Delano & Aldrich designed Monahan Gymnasium (1938), which Pennoyer and others rallied to preserve for adaptive reuse.

Much in the same way PPA treats the New York City streetscape as a contextual guide, it embraces the history and the idiosyncrasies of site to inform its work outside Manhattan. A Catskills retreat completed in 1990 for the late writer Louis Auchincloss and his artist wife, Adele, established Pennoyer and his partners' ability to evoke an extraordinary sense of place. Conceived as a simple vernacular building—or in the words of Auchincloss, "almost a carpenter's structure"—inspired by Gunnar Asplund's Villa Snellman, the house gives the impression of being civilized by classical accents—"at once formal and toy-like, diffident and playful," according to architectural critic Paul Goldberger. Inside, a top-lit, two-story library with a circular inner balcony rises through the center, creating a private yet open refuge for writing. A new house for Pennoyer's parents on Mishaum Point on Buzzard's Bay in southeastern Massachusetts from 1991 captures a different tradition—one that Pennoyer knows well. He spent his summers in this community in a Shingle Style family house designed by William Ralph Emerson at the turn of the twentieth century. Aspects of this house fed into the new design, informing its basic massing, orientation, and low outstretching veranda so evocative of summer living. From Stern, Pennoyer took the idea that a house design begins by suggesting a way of living. With an emphasis on the relationship of rooms, their rhythm, balance, comfort, and flow, PPA carefully sculpts the interior architecture of a house. By finessing the relationship among plan, elevation, and section, the firm effectively tailors space, controls volume, and configures circulation to shape the client's experience. In this capacity, all of PPA's houses—and classical architecture in general—echo human movement and incorporate time-tested traditional forms that respond to environment factors. Well rooted in the landscape, they are positive contributions—beautiful and built to last.

The fluidity and inventive spirit of the firm's work reflects the collegial but intense focus found in the studio at the heart of the office. At the core of the practice are Pennoyer's

ABOVE

A virtual model of the east portico of Drumlin Hall calculates the movement and effect of the sun.

ABOVE LEFT

A new Shingle Style house on Mishaum Point in southeastern Massachusetts absorbs the history and vernacular of the area in a new and fresh way by combining low spreading porches, shingles, and a gabled roof with an asymmetrical oriel window and arched French doors.

longtime friends and colleagues, partner Thomas P. R. Nugent and Gregory Gilmartin, director of design, as well as partner Elizabeth Graziolo, a graduate of Cooper Union. Each project exists as a collaboration among the draftsman and architects who not only excel at time-honored methods of design and presentation, such as watercolor and pen-and-ink perspectives, but also the most advanced computer design tools. Proficiency in 3-D modeling and animation programs enables the firm to create virtual models to test design concepts, calculate the movement and effect of the sun, and render projects. At the same time, the fundamental importance of drawing has not been lost. As Pennoyer maintains, the physical act of sketching with a pencil and paper trains the mind to see and understand a design in a way that cannot be translated into a series of computer commands. Exquisite watercolors by the Russian-born Anton Glikin, a graduate of the St. Petersburg Academy of Fine Arts and The Prince of Wales's Institute of Architecture, present new projects in yet another dimension. PPA also enjoys fruitful relationships with a number of interior decorators; landscape architects; and a variety of designers, craftsmen, and artists.

PPA's creative process starts from the ground up; the firm considers each project a research challenge, with the final solution resting on a profound appreciation for and thorough knowledge of history. The library, which houses over 4,500 volumes, both current and rare, is the setting for some of the practice's most productive research. This comprehensive command of the past informs the firm's design approach. Rather than simply reproducing examples from pattern books, PPA engages the influence of architectural history and uses it as a springboard for interpretive and imaginative work. Thus, the work of such British greats as Sir John Soane, Robert Adam, Robert Taylor, C. R. Cockerell, and Thomas Leverton and American masters Stanford White, Mott Schmidt, William Adams Delano, Charles Platt, and Harrie T. Lindeberg—all architects that PPA admires—become a bottomless reserve of inspiration.

At Diamond A Ranch, Meadow Lane House, and Oakley Farm—renovations and additions to existing houses—or with new construction, such as Adirondack Camp, House in the Santa Lucia Range, and House on Penobscot Bay, PPA demonstrates its stylistic range. From

the weathered Shingle Style of New England to the Arts and Crafts tradition of the Pacific coast, PPA absorbs the history and the vernacular of an area and reworks and remakes it to become its own. But, as a reflection of its versatility, the firm is just as astute in designing a purely classical house. The recently completed Drumlin Hall in Dutchess County, New York, is a modern-day version of a Palladian villa—a house that revels in perfect proportion, rigorous geometry, and the great flexibility of the classical idiom. Set in a valley of miniature hills, at first glance it seems to be an English house built ages ago. Designed to set off important collections of art and furniture, Drumlin Hall culminates twenty years of PPA's practice in a moment when the client's voice; the firm's creative talent; and the contributions of interior decorators, artists, and master craftsmen unite. Larger-scaled schemes for a neoclassical limestone house on the North Shore of Long Island and a Manhattan townhouse, containing a stylistically eclectic suite of classical rooms effectively refined and knit together, continue in the classical vein. Each project luxuriates in an extraordinary attention to the smallest of details and the subtle nuances and threads of architectural history inventively distilled and fluidly interwoven into the design. As William Adams Delano once said, "I am a strong believer in tradition, but tradition tempered with motion." With each project, PPA embodies in bricks and mortar its understanding of beauty, making its dreams tangible. In the increasingly fragmented field of architecture, with one extreme embracing the various permutations of modernism, the self-consciously avant-garde, and the other constructing the traditional American dream house, the work of PPA continues to be powerfully anchored in a strain of classicism that, having shed the irony of postmodernism, strikes an equilibrium between comfort, luxury, and understated beauty.

ABOVE

A watercolor of a large neoclassical house on Long Island reflects the storied history and grand-estate era of the North Shore.

ABOVE RIGHT

A laylight at Drumlin Hall demonstrates an extraordinary attention to detail and subtle beauty.

OPPOSITE

In restoring and renovating Diamond A Ranch, the firm layered styles across the complex, weaving a historical narrative of New Mexico's architectural heritage, including adding this new colonnaded patio to unify the space and embrace the landscape.

APARTMENTS

FIFTH AVENUE TRIPLEX

ABOVE
Framed by an elliptical arch, the stair off the sitting room is lit from the penthouse above.

OPPOSITE
Paneled arched openings scaled to each room frame the view of Central Park in the living room.

THIS TRIPLEX OCCUPIES THE TOP THREE FLOORS OF A SEVEN-apartment, fifteen-floor cooperative on Manhattan's Fifth Avenue set on a narrow twenty-five-foot-wide lot. Designed by I. N. Phelps Stokes in 1924, the building is located on the type of site traditionally reserved for a house and features charming and compact apartments with unusual plans and quirky space-saving elements, such as narrow hallways and stairs, pocket doors, and rooms that connect through one another rather than being separated by halls. Few residential buildings on the Upper East Side possess such a footprint; it is the narrowest Fifth Avenue lot ever to be developed with a tall apartment house.

An heir to the Phelps Dodge mining fortune, Stokes was an architect, historian, and developer primarily concerned with low-income housing reform. Much of his enthusiasm and inheritance, including the money he made on this project, was funneled into what became his lifelong passion: the creation of the six-volume *Iconography of Manhattan Island, 1498–1909,* an exhaustive study of the development of Manhattan from the sixth century to the early twentieth century. So much time and money went into the project that Stokes could no longer afford his seventh-and-eighth-floor duplex in this building overlooking Central Park.

The narrowness of the site not only sets this apartment apart from other grand Upper East Side apartments but also presented a challenge in the design process. The width of the plan, which contracts to thirteen feet at the back of the apartment, creates an intimacy more synonymous with a house—albeit one in the sky with luxurious views of the cityscape. The large front rooms, each lit by three windows overlooking the park (the lower two floors also have a fourth window looking south) are generously scaled to the width of the building; however, the spaces became somewhat cramped through its one hundred–foot depth, leaving little leeway for change or separation between rooms. But unlike most townhouses, which are generally open only to the front and rear, this apartment has windows along the southern exposure—a benefit created by several shorter houses and apartments next door.

PPA redesigned the interior architecture and the stair to exude a sensuality that only full-bodied traditional details, moldings, and casings can create. In addition, the firm

RIGHT

The suede-paneled sitting room on the top floor opens out to terraces on the east and west.

reengineered the space and reframed the steel on the upper part of the building. This allowed PPA to open up the rooms and create a clear axis through them. The small, light-filled, south-facing entry vestibule opens to the east into a new oak-paneled Tudor style dining room inspired by the room's original leaded glass casement. This room connects back to the kitchen to the east. A newly opened enfilade framed by broad elliptical arches stretches west from the vestibule through a sitting room into the large formal living room. Because the room sizes were limited by the building's width, PPA linked the rooms with telescoping arches that broaden and lengthen as they move toward Fifth Avenue. While properly scaled to each room, they tie the interconnected spaces together and create the optical illusion that they are the same size.

In the living room, which was eclectically decorated—as was the entire apartment—by Katie Leede, smooth walls create a calm background to set off the clients' collection of American art, including works by Childe Hassam, Winslow Homer, Maurice Prendergast, and Gilbert Stuart. The sitting room, which PPA expanded by eliminating a hall, acquires a new sense of compositional order created by its circular tray ceiling and broad arched entrances. Since the stair opening could not be expanded, the design of the new streamlined stair also posed a challenge. And although it was constructed using high-tech computer numeric control methods, it fits with the apartment's traditional style and appears as though it was built decades ago by skilled craftsmen. However, the elliptical arch under which the stair curves up to the second-level bedrooms—rather than the stair itself—is what successfully creates the illusion of a full-bodied curvature in keeping with the architectural language of the apartment. On the top floor, a suede-paneled aerie connects to terraces to the east and west and enjoys spectacular views of the park and the tower of the Carlyle Hotel, an iconic presence in the Manhattan skyline.

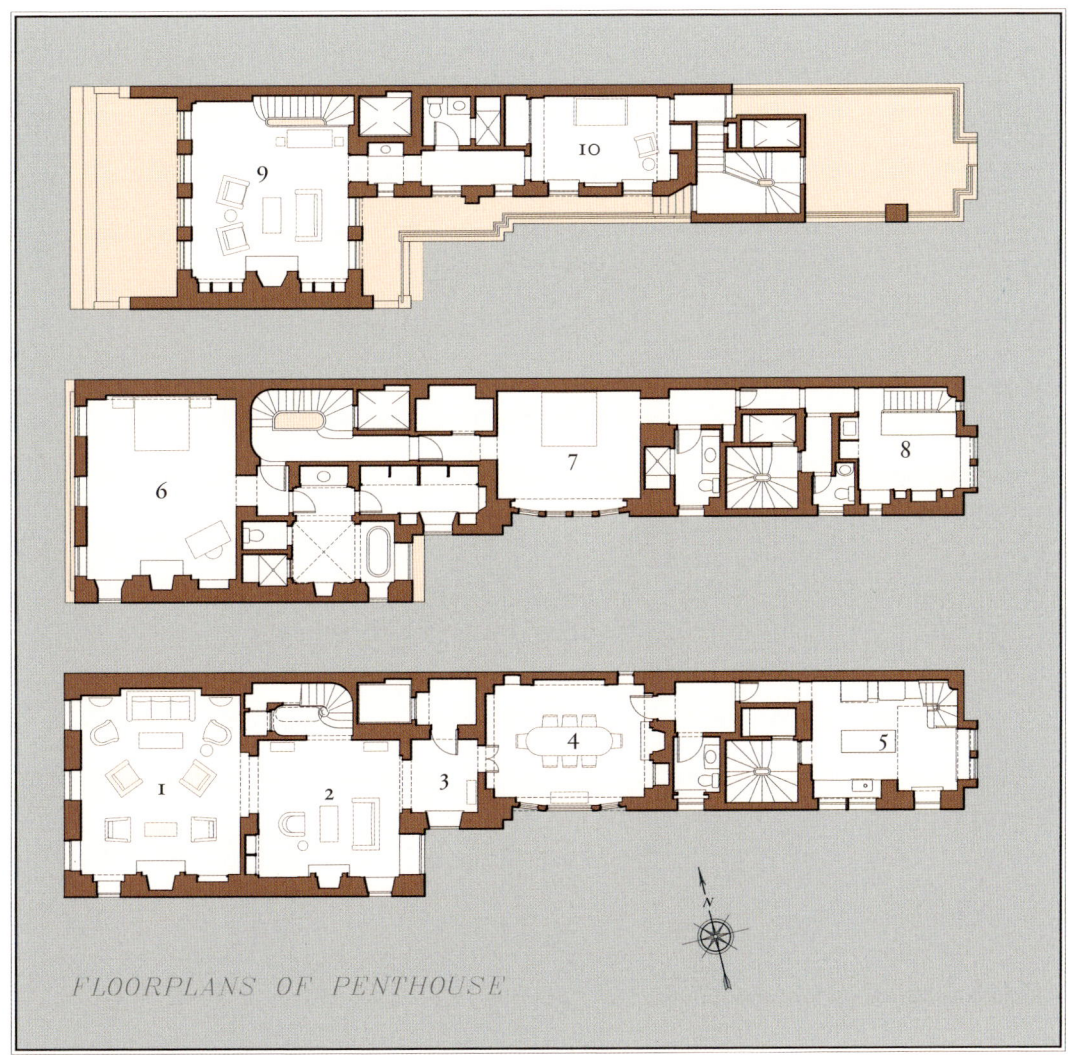

FLOORPLANS OF PENTHOUSE

PLAN

The plan narrows toward the east, allowing south facing windows.

1. Living room
2. Sitting room
3. Foyer
4. Dining room
5. Kitchen
6. Master bedroom
7. Bedroom
8. Laundry
9. Sitting room
10. Study

BELOW

The copper facade of the penthouse faces Central Park.

FIFTH AVENUE TRIPLEX ❖ 33

OPPOSITE

The enfilade of rooms provides a vista from the living room through the sitting room and into the dining room.

NORTH ELEVATION

On the paneled north wall of the dining room, new sculptural frames mark two original leaded windows.

BELOW

Leaded-glass windows and doors and oak paneling bring Tudor details in to the dining room.

FIFTH AVENUE TRIPLEX

ABOVE

The master bathroom was inspired by an eccentric English mantel, which is framed by a groin vault.

RIGHT

To carve the most space from the narrow footprint, the stair transitions directly into the penthouse sitting room, where suede wall panels reflect the shallow coffered ceiling.

EAST SIDE DUPLEX

BELOW
The living room mantel was modeled on the abstract classical forms of French designer André Arbus.

OPPOSITE
Overlapping the entrance to the living room, the stair floats in the hall, asserting a sculptural presence.

Located in a historic, fourteen-story limestone Delano & Aldrich building built between 1907 and 1909, this apartment makes up part of two floors in one of the first luxury apartment houses on Park Avenue. McKim, Mead & White's 998 Fifth Avenue and Warren & Wetmore's 903 Park Avenue, two of the area's most sumptuous early buildings, were completed several years later. Despite its august pedigree as an early attempt at high-rise living, the building was executed well before the concept had been embraced and hence the apartment had many awkward features. To create a modern, comfortable, and technologically up-to-date living space for a large family, PPA tempered the plan and reworked the interior architecture to reflect the clients' contemporary tastes.

Each floor of the building originally consisted of three duplex apartments and a diminutive single-floor bachelor's apartment in the rear. In this project, two apartments—a duplex with three bedrooms and several small servants' rooms and one of the small rear simplexes on the upper level—were combined. While the layout of the first floor essentially remained the same, the upper level was reconfigured: staff rooms were combined into a second-floor playroom and the back apartment was transformed into an extension of the master suite. Already altered by dated renovations, the apartment had been stripped of many of the original moldings, but retained its eclectic original mantels and a wood sidewinding stair with a Colonial Revival handrail.

In the redesign of the interiors, PPA reworked some of the awkward plan features to create rooms that evoke the openness of a loft. In the original plan, the kitchen and servants' rooms faced onto Park Avenue, an unusual layout for a luxury apartment where these amenities are usually buried in the rear. This naive plan turned out to be a great asset, bringing light and views into the kitchen, one of the apartment's most heavily used spaces. PPA reconfigured doorways to open new axes and generate a new interconnectedness through the rooms, in one case creating an unexpected enfilade of double doors from the living room through the dining room and into the formerly closed off kitchen to link the public and private spheres. This new openness between rooms promotes their use as functional living spaces. The sunlit kitchen and adjoining nook—used as an office area—had previously been cramped

and disjointed. The firm's new design incorporating sleek millwork, a stainless steel and glass range hood, and terrazzo floor gives it a clean, sophisticated feeling. Repositioning one of the living room walls produced the opportunity for an octagonal, lacquered-wood-paneled library.

PPA emphasized a stripped and abstracted aesthetic to underscore the apartment's streamlined expression. In the entry hall, the firm encased two original freestanding piers inside a broad arched opening, increased door heights, and expanded the stair opening,

BELOW
The bronze balustrade is a whimsical interpretation of traditional form.

PLAN

New openings create an enfilade along the west side of the apartment.

1. Entry hall
2. Library
3. Living room
4. Dining room
5. Kitchen
6. Pantry
7. Office

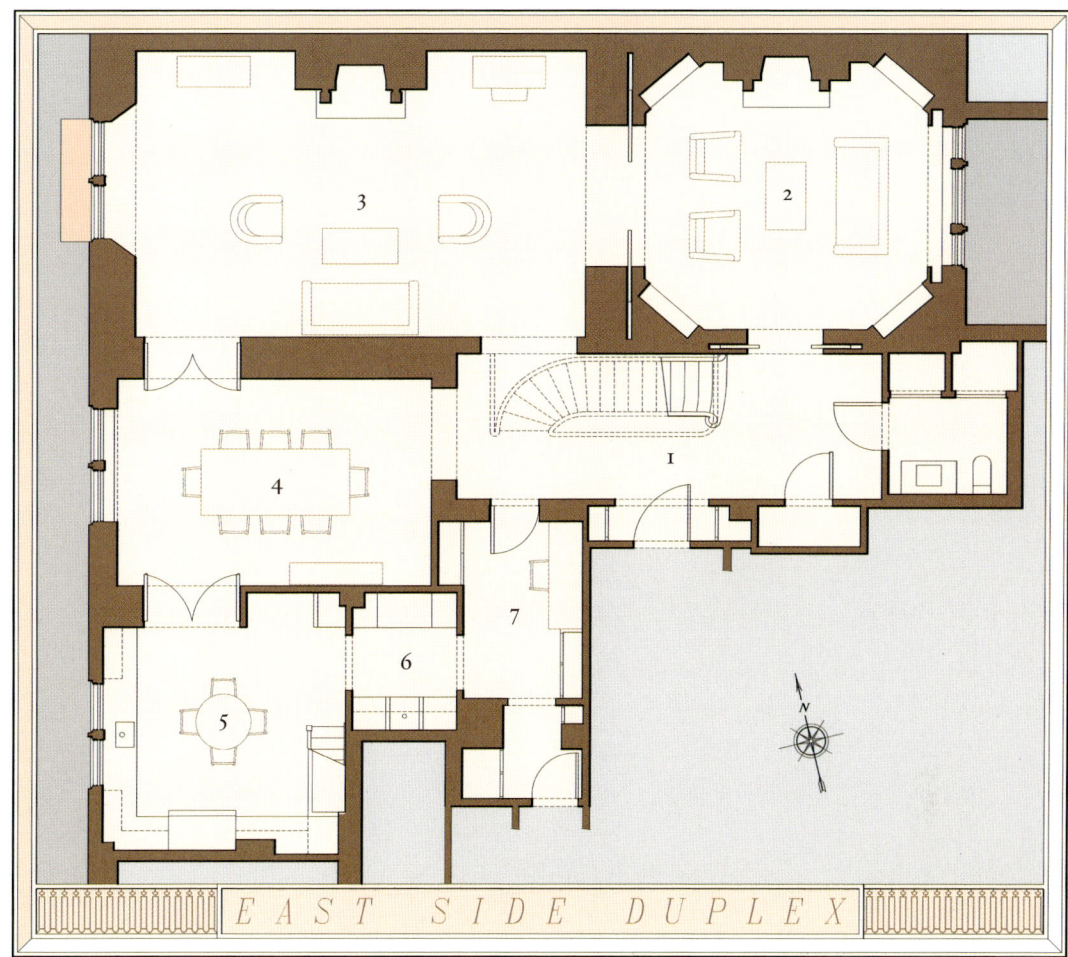

creating new site lines and vantage points from one room to another. The new stair pulls away from the wall to allow light to filter from the upper level. With its gentle sweep, abstracted bronze balustrade, and mahogany handrail, it becomes a freestanding sculptural object. While all of the rooms are classically proportioned, the design is light and sparing. Newly designed mantels embellished with distilled classical details in the living room and master bedroom replace the original heavier off-the-shelf elements of Chester Aldrich's design. Flat ceilings with crown moldings replaced the exposed beams.

Eve Robinson's decoration in shades of brown, blue, and silver complements the luxurious understatement of the design and creates the ideal backdrop for the clients' collections of photography and sculpture. Throughout, dark Brazilian cherry floors contribute to the crisp minimalist atmosphere of the public rooms. The private spaces, particularly the children's bathrooms, are sleek and modern while the Moderne master dressing area features cove moldings, inset leather panels, crystal-accented hardware, and crystal-beaded wall covering. From the kitchen, a back stair leads up to what were formerly staff quarters. PPA combined a series of small rooms into a new playroom, where clear doors patterned with bamboo and glossy white built-ins accented with dark brown give the once-outdated space a fresh and contemporary expression.

ABOVE

The bolection-form mantelpiece centers the octagonal paneled library.

RIGHT

An enfilade linked by double doors creates an unexpected axis from the living room through the dining room to the kitchen.

BELOW

Expansive windows opened at the rear of the apartment bathe the new mantel wall in the master bedroom in eastern light.

ABOVE
The door to the back stair brings whimsy to the playroom with patterned bamboo rings encased in glass; this is continued in the room by asymmetrical white and brown painted cabinetry for toys.

ABOVE RIGHT
A compact back stair rises behind the sunlit kitchen.

RIGHT
Panels in the dressing room feature lacquered surfaces, glass-bead wallpaper, mirrors, and leather.

PARK AVENUE APARTMENT

I**N THE RENOVATION OF THIS PARK AVENUE APARTMENT, LOCATED IN A** historic limestone building designed by York & Sawyer in 1927, PPA transported the glamour and cosmopolitan spirit of French design into a contemporary, family-friendly living space. Both principals of York & Sawyer, Edward York and Philip Sawyer, trained in the office of McKim, Mead & White. While they were best known for their loosely modeled, classically inspired banks—especially their Florentine-style building for the Federal Reserve Bank—they were, like the best firms of the day, skillful at designing just about anything from clubs (New York Athletic Club) to museums (New-York Historical Society), churches (Brick Presbyterian Church), and private houses. In this apartment building, one of the firm's few, they constructed a pared-down but enlarged version of an Italian Renaissance palazzo and filled it with generously scaled apartments with large rooms and lofty ceilings. Each of the building's eleven apartments—with the exception of one large triplex maisonette—occupies a floor, but unlike the others in the building, this apartment possesses a shallow terrace and a series of French doors opening onto Park Avenue.

The clients admired the work of French architects and designers such as André Arbus, Jean-Charles Moreux, and Jean-Michel Frank, and wanted PPA to translate something of their stripped-down Art Deco essence into the new design. Like most New Yorkers, they also desired ample storage and a maximum use of the space. Reconfiguring circulation and arranging rooms is a strength of PPA; the firm finessed the plan, initiating a seamless flow between spaces and adapting the apartment to twenty-first-century living. For example, the kitchen, pantry, and staff quarters—a sequence of small, antiquated rooms—were combined into a large open kitchen as well as a playroom off of the entrance gallery. Similarly, the master suite and adjoining dressing areas and bathrooms were more fluidly arranged. In the public rooms PPA established a strong central axis extending from the library through the living room and into the dining room, offsetting the slight asymmetry of the dining room. By using double doors throughout, the firm was able to open up and interlink the spaces.

Meanwhile, the firm's architectural finishes give rise to the apartment's cosmopolitan French character and infuse it with light, accentuating the clients' modern art collection. PPA sought to emphasize the dramatic effect of the uncommonly high ceilings and the

OPPOSITE

Dramatic pocket doors in black lacquer inlaid with geometric patterns in nickel open into the dining room, creating a sophisticated contrast of dark and light.

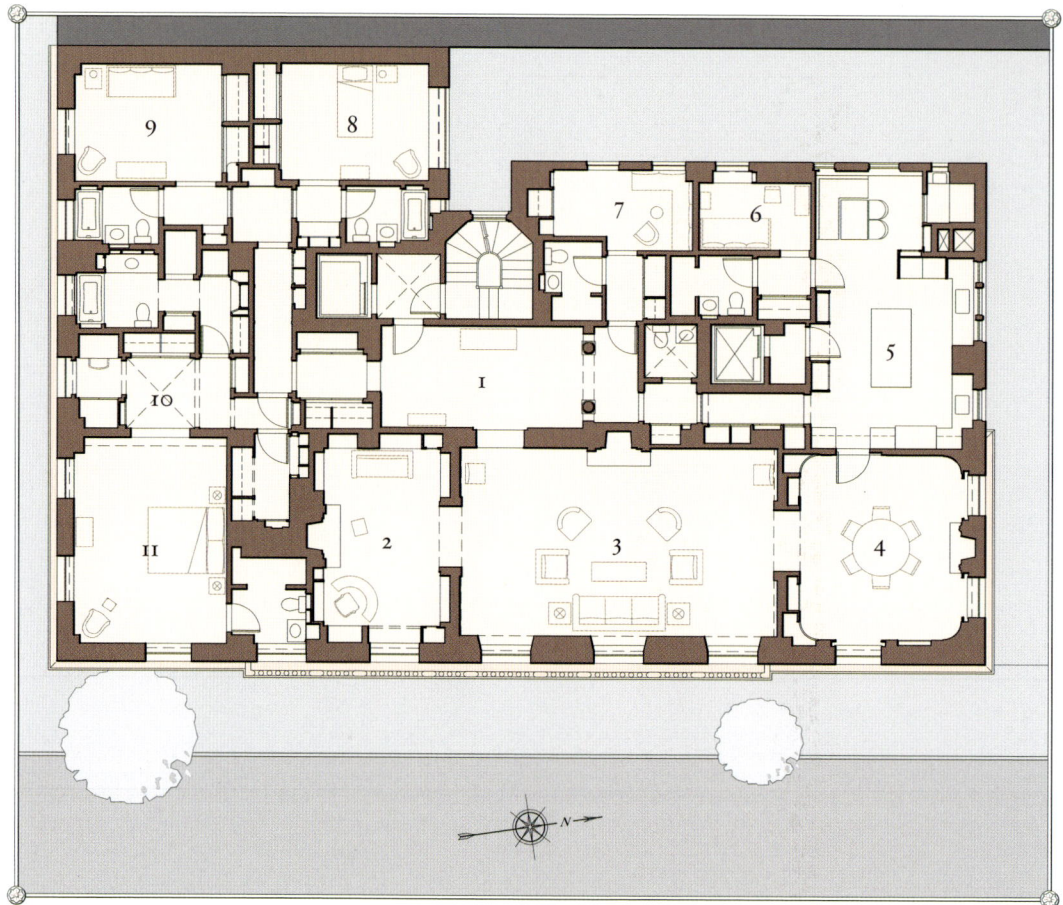

ABOVE

The Greek-key frieze in this groin-vaulted, mother-of-pearl-paneled bathroom is actually a fretwork grille concealing the exhaust system.

PLAN

Major rooms face a balcony to the east fronting Park Avenue.

1. Foyer
2. Library
3. Living room
4. Dining room
5. Kitchen
6. Bedroom
7. Playroom
8. Bedroom
9. Bedroom
10. Dressing room
11. Master bedroom

OPPOSITE

In the foyer, the inlaid floor patterns in marble and nickel and the stylized metal door reflect the stripped-down Art Deco character of the apartment.

floor-to-ceiling French doors in the living room and library—the apartment's most unusual feature. In the doors, large panes of glass and the thin profiles of the muntins allow for an abundance of light to pass through, a quality that is reinforced by the white oak floors and a glazed service door in the dining room. In the foyer, PPA gave the long gallery a sense of compositional order and gravity by incorporating two full-bodied Doric columns, limestone floors inset with stylized strips of marble and nickel, and a front door embellished with an abstracted ironwork pattern. Like the floor, black lacquered doors detailed with nickel in both the foyer and the dining room create a bold and sophisticated contrast reminiscent of Dorothy Draper's design aesthetic. Off the entrance gallery a new powder room with mother-of-pearl walls, vaulted ceiling, and Greek key banding—which cleverly masks the exhaust system—stands as a tiny jewel box. In the dining room, lacquered wood paneling, curved walls, and a pewter-leaf foiled ceiling evoke the atmosphere of a *hôtel particulier*, but a stripped-down mantel set on axis with that of the cerused-oak-paneled library gives the room a more contemporary feel. Here, every nook and cranny of the space is used; cabinets are seamlessly set behind the streamlined curves of the paneling. Throughout the apartment, custom built-ins and millwork—in the dressing areas, children's rooms and hall, and kitchen—provide storage while decoration by David Kleinberg, distilled moldings and casings, French hardware, stylized grilles, glazed doors, and vaults reinforce the design's Art Deco–influenced French expression.

OPPOSITE

Cabinets are seamlessly incorporated into the paneling and curved walls of the dining room.

RIGHT

The library was built with boiserie (carved wood panels) in cerused oak, a brushed white finish that fills the porous grain of the dark-stained wood; popular in the Art Deco period, it heightens the contrast between dark and light.

BELOW

Door frames engage the cornice in the soaring living room, where white oak floors and tall windows brighten the space.

FAR LEFT

The bathroom, strapped in contrasting stone, overlooks Park Avenue and a shallow terrace.

LEFT

A niche fitted with a writing table brings south light into the vaulted dressing room.

BELOW

The arched entrance to the master bedroom aligns with mirrored closet doors in the dressing room beyond.

OPPOSITE

In the kitchen, a light box is incorporated into the range hood and the André Arbus–inspired light fixtures reflect the room's sleek minimalism.

EAST RIVER APARTMENT

IN THE PUBLIC ROOMS OF THIS APARTMENT OVERLOOKING MANHATTAN'S East River, PPA channeled English and Moorish influences to develop an original and stylized design aesthetic that was glamorous for parties, restrained to showcase the clients' art collection, and comfortable for daily living. The dramatic entryway sets the stage for the fusion of these three purposes. The large gallery connecting the front door and foyer to the living and dining rooms acts as the hinge of the plan and is boldly expressed. The fluted plaster walls—inset with beads and distilled floral motifs—produce a stylized texture while the floor's circle-and-square pattern of portoro and calacatta gold marbles, fashioned after ancient Roman models, lends the effect of entering into a palace.

A pair of black lacquered pocket doors opens into a silk-lined dining room enhanced by a full-bodied ornamental plaster ceiling carved with motifs inspired by the floor patterns of Sir Edwin Lutyens's work in New Delhi; here PPA cleverly masked the air vents as a chain of small abstracted medallions set into the curve of its ellipse. The firm designed the sun-drenched living room to fit the scale of the fluted Regency mantel embellished with Greek keys designed by Sir John Soane. While the intimate adjoining library is finished in red leather and waxed white oak, white walls throughout create a neutral setting to highlight art. Beak-and-bead casings and base and crown moldings add a layer of polish and voluptuousness to the rooms, decorated by Michael S. Smith, and a sumptuous palette of materials, including different marbles, gold and silver leaf, embossed leather, and matte gold-plated hardware, reinforce the apartment's tasteful opulence. In the powder room, artist Nancy Lorenz erected gold panels with a relief of abstract bamboo within the framework of the moldings.

This apartment is located in an elegant and historic building that was developed in 1925 by the children of Henry Phipps, Andrew Carnegie's partner in the Carnegie Steel Company, and designed in partnership by the gifted apartment specialist Rosario Candela and the Beaux-Arts–trained firm of Cross & Cross. With the exception of a great rooftop simplex, most floors are occupied by a duplex flanked by two large apartments. This apartment in the north wing has expansive river views, exceptional light, and four exposures, a feature enabled by the building's U-shaped plan. Essentially

OPPOSITE

The gilded ellipse of the raised decorative ceiling in the dining room is anchored with guilloche, the ceiling ornament of interlace bands.

BELOW

The fluted plaster walls in the gallery, inset with beads and floral motifs at the level of a traditional chair rail, create a dramatic effect.

a rectangle with the elevator core at its center, it originally had four large bedrooms, a series of maids' rooms, kitchen, pantry, servants' hall, and the requisite public spaces, including an unusually large entrance gallery. As is typical in its apartment renovations, PPA upgraded the many small rooms with outdated functions; this included relocating the kitchen to give it a river view and combining the narrow maids' rooms into guest and media rooms and a nursery. To create an ample and comfortable master suite, the firm organized an enfilade including a bedroom, sitting room, and dressing rooms, and boudoir.

In plan, PPA successfully established a division between the apartment's public and private realms. Off of the foyer, the hallway leading to the master suite and guest room was widened to display art but broken into two distinct vestibules. The first accesses the powder room, while the later and more private portion has the ability to

BELOW
The gallery floor, inlaid with calacatta gold and portoro marbles, was inspired by a traditional Roman pattern.

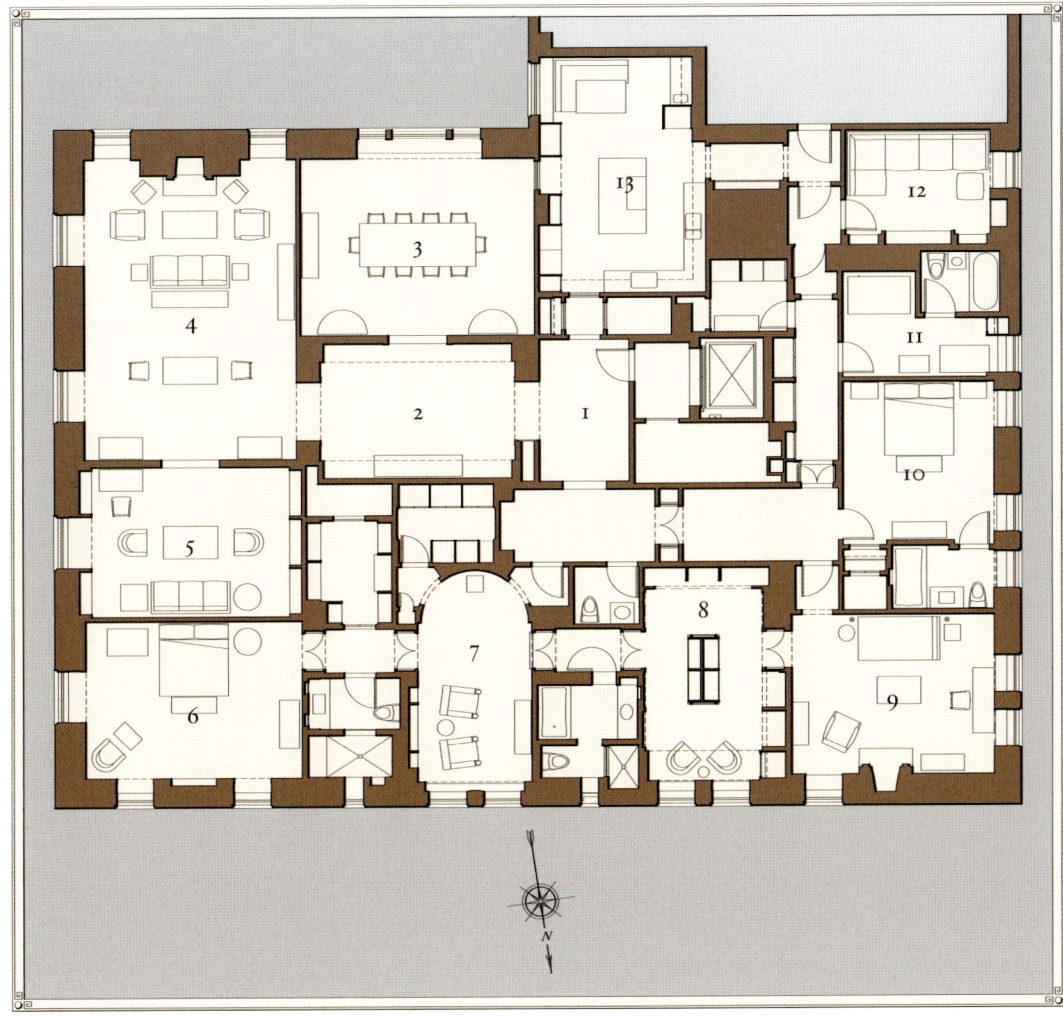

PLAN

The gallery, at the center of the plan, connects the foyer to the public rooms.

1. Foyer
2. Gallery
3. Dining room
4. Living room
5. Library
6. Master bedroom
7. Sitting room
8. Dressing room
9. Boudoir
10. Guest room
11. Nursery
12. Media room
13. Kitchen

OVERLEAF

Stylized crown moldings and bolection casings give an Anglo-Moroccan character to the sun-drenched living room, scaled around a mantel designed by Sir John Soane.

be closed off during parties. In the master suite, the large dressing room and bath stand as highlights. A series of mirrors inset into arches—stripped-down versions of those inspired by the Moorish mosques of Córdoba, Spain—line the walls and a thin coffered ceiling detailed with beads instills the room with femininity. While the composition of the adjoining bathroom is relatively reserved, it luxuriates in the use of rosa aurora marble, rock crystal, mirrors, and poured glass moldings, materials that unleash its lavish cosmopolitan expression. In the former servants' hall, the firm gave the previously humble area an architectural identity, creating an unexpected jewel box of barrel vaults, grilles, and moldings designed to balance the rhythm of the various doors that open off the corridor.

OPPOSITE
Black lacquered pocket doors open from the light-colored living room into a library of waxed white-oak paneling with a stained oak floor.

TOP RIGHT
The east-facing kitchen features strapping on the ceiling and walls, a ribbed-glass and stainless-steel hood, calacatta gold marble countertop and floor, and a corner banquette.

RIGHT
Black lacquered plaster stiles and rails and black and gold portoro marble floors set off Nancy Lorenz's gold relief panels in the powder room.

TOWNHOUSES

CARNEGIE HILL BROWNSTONE

BELOW
A new neo-Federal garden facade steps back to create terraces.

OPPOSITE
The vaulted second-floor library leads to the family room facing the garden.

OVER THE PAST CENTURY, THE ARCHITECTURE OF THIS SLENDER, eighteen-foot-wide brownstone located in the heart of the Carnegie Hill Historic District had been significantly debased. A holdover from the speculative building boom at the end of the nineteenth century, when the streets of Carnegie Hill were developed as rows of houses, it was built by the architectural firm A. B. Ogden & Son in 1886 as one of four Queen Anne–style houses for Andrew J. Kerwin, a real estate operator credited with the invention of the kitchenette. During the first half of the twentieth century, the house was divided into apartments, its emblematic brownstone stoop was removed, and its parlor-floor windows were enlarged and shifted to reflect the reconfigured rooms inside. While various architects had tried to relieve the monotony of these strips of brownstones during the early years of the 1900s by removing stoops and designing new street facades in variations of Georgian, Tudor, and French styles, this particular house stood mainly as a degraded version of its former self. In restoring it to a single house, PPA reconstructed the entire building down to the party walls, creating an utterly new house set between a restored street facade and a newly designed garden facade. The firm's approach, in adapting the house to the modern needs of a family, focused on differentiating and distinguishing an otherwise thin and unremarkable brownstone. What could have been a straightforward renovation of a conventional building type with a predictable plan and section was translated into a moment of inspired design innovation.

Working under the regulations of the New York Landmarks Preservation Commission, PPA preserved the historic spirit of the well-worn street facade. Lost brownstone details were reestablished, such as the carved window and door surrounds at the ground and parlor levels, which were modeled after the existing original window frames on the upper stories. The street level, which formerly consisted of an enlarged window sandwiched between two unaligned entrances, was redesigned to fit the eighteen-foot width of the house more agilely and to create a more appropriate entrance. Since the garden facade was visible at street level, through an alley on the next street, it was also subject to design review by the Landmarks Preservation Commission. Formerly a hodgepodge of additions built deeper into the garden than current codes allow, this elevation presented a chance to create

PLAN

The north and south flights of stairs connect at a central landing on the second floor.

1. Living room
2. Library
3. Sitting room
4. Breakfast room
5. Kitchen
6. Hall
7. Foyer
8. Study

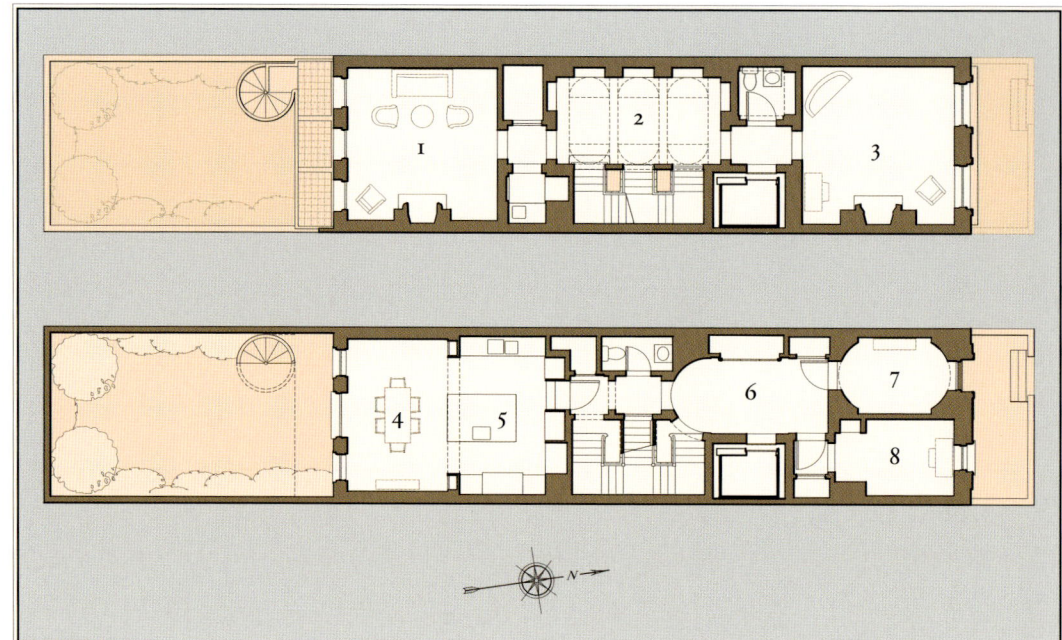

something new. Rather than carrying over elements from the front, the firm designed an elegant red-brick and stone neo-Federal facade with terraces on the setbacks and stairs from the second floor spiraling down to the restored rear garden area designed by Maureen Hackett. The rooftop addition, which expanded the building to five stories and 5,000 square feet, was also subject to review; PPA contextually designed it to recede and to be undetectable from the street, winning the support of the local civic group.

While preservation guidelines and parameters controlled the outcome of the exterior, the interiors, decorated by Matthew Smyth in cool shades of blues and browns, could adhere less to custom. In some cases, the slim dimensions of the house may have been limiting; here, they only add to its allure and charm. Rooms, at once well proportioned and livable, are accessibly sized to a young and growing family. Following the plan of a typical English basement townhouse, a single room opens to the front and to the rear with the stair—which PPA relocated from the side of the building—at its core. With this repositioning came the hinge of the design and, unpredictable from the brownstone's facade, the architectural surprise. From the ground floor foyer, an atypical double stretch of stair ascends to the parlor level. Here it leads into a vaulted library, inspired by James Wyatt's Heveningham Hall, which runs along the transverse axis and is flanked to the north by a formal sitting room and to the south by a living room with three arched French doors leading out to the terrace. With its stylish Art Deco circular grilles, walls of books, glossy ribbing, and series of three arches along the east wall that articulate the stair sequence, the library becomes the unexpected aesthetic treat and the heart of the house. As the stair extends to the bedroom levels under a pared-down laylight, the architecture of the upper floors becomes more stripped down and almost abstract in effect, reflecting contemporary tastes.

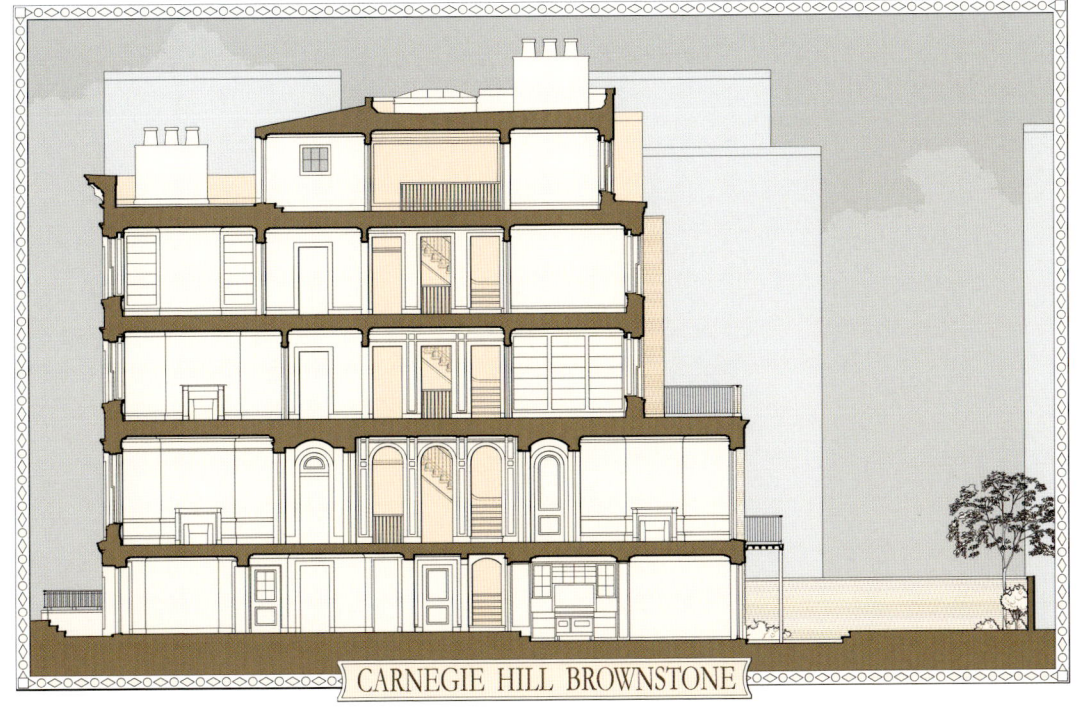

CARNEGIE HILL BROWNSTONE

SECTION
The stair, relocated to the core of the house, ascends under the fifth-floor laylight.

BELOW
The east wall of the second-floor library is articulated as a sequence of arches that embraces the stair.

LEFT
Oversized arched doors bring light and views into the living room and open out to a glass-floored terrace overlooking the garden.

TOP
The kitchen and breakfast room face onto the garden.

ABOVE
The cornice in the sitting room is fluted to capture the soaring height of the space.

ABOVE AND BELOW
The design of the vaults in the library was studied in a digital model. The vaults were peeled up to the arched form of the shelves.

OPPOSITE RIGHT

An early study of the living room incorporated vaults similar to those in the library.

LEFT

The stair ascends beneath a stripped-down laylight on the fifth floor.

BELOW

The central flight of steps at the second floor crosses the well of the stairs.

BEAUX-ARTS TOWNHOUSE

I N 1901 AND 1902, WHEN OVER TWO HUNDRED TOWNHOUSES WERE built on New York's Upper East Side by a number of Beaux Arts–trained architects, the streets of the newly fashionable residential district were transformed by a host of classically inspired designs. The sculptural brick-and-limestone facade of this Beaux-Arts–style house in the Upper East Side Historic District, designed in 1902 by Charles Brendon for William G. Park, director of the Crucible Steel Company, embodies the essence of the French taste in vogue at the turn of the twentieth century. Over time, many radical interior alterations had obliterated the historic fabric. In embarking on what was essentially an entirely new 7,500-square-foot building behind the preserved street facade, PPA contemplated a design approach for the interiors that would best complement and encapsulate the lively and distinctive spirit of its primary elevation.

Meanwhile, on the exterior, the firm restored the facade to full color with repointed brick, a combination of restored and new ironwork, and a new Mansard roof clad in verdigris-painted sheet metal. To reestablish the attic dormer and balustrade, which had been obscured by additions, PPA reinterpreted what would have originally existed to design an appropriate and contextual solution. In contrast, the garden facade was carried out with little ornament save Flemish bond brickwork and stone band courses. To open up the garden and maximize space, the firm removed a protruding wing and extended the footprint of the twenty-one-foot-wide house flush to the thirty-foot garden limit. The small formal garden was enclosed with a stone parapeted brick wall and latticework fence, and a decorative cast stone double stair was added to connect the outdoor space to the eat-in kitchen at street level. The caretaker's apartment in the basement is accessed by a run of steps set beneath its steep arch.

Because the plan template of a townhouse is generally fixed with one room to the front and one to the rear, the interior architecture differentiates one house from the next. Here, the emblematic street facade established the tone; the architecture of the rooms, which were decorated by the client, takes its cues from the French. However, unlike the exuberant exterior, the classical language of the rooms is more refined—as a reflection of modern taste—and does not seek to emulate the full-blown baroque elements that most

OPPOSITE

A column screen frames the upper staircase on the third floor.

BELOW

The original Beaux-Arts facade of the townhouse was restored.

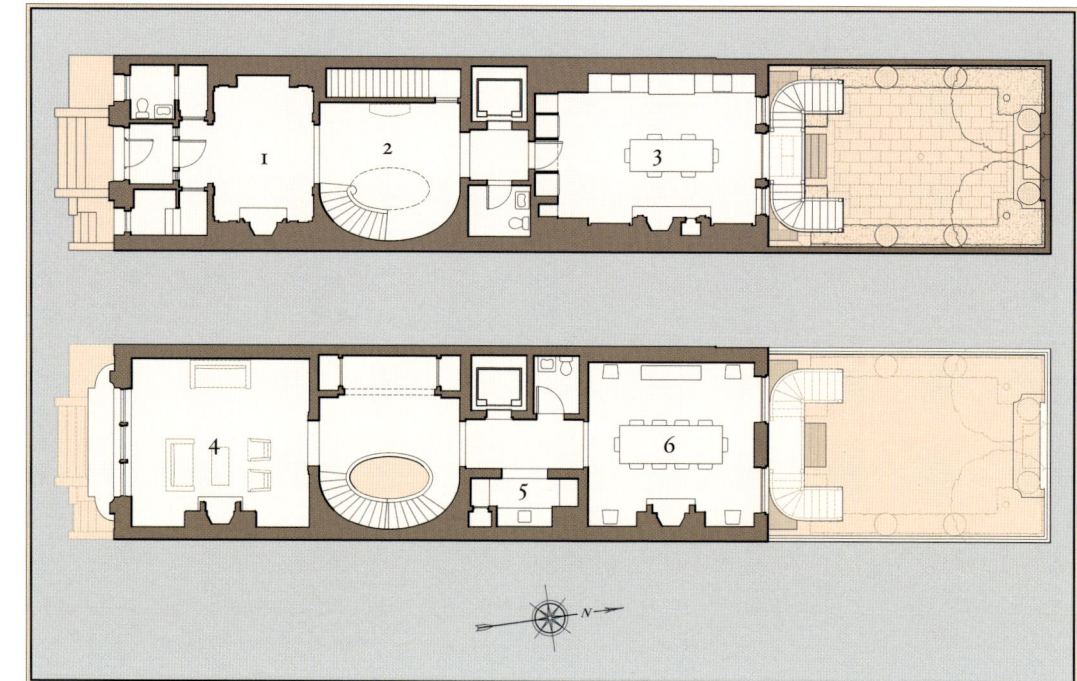

PLAN

The semielliptical stair hall occupies the center of the floor plan.

1. Entry hall
2. Stair hall
3. Kitchen
4. South parlor
5. Butler's pantry
6. Dining room

SECTION

This townhouse displays a typical layout of two rooms per floor, divided by a stair. The architectural elements within the traditional townhouse template, refined and distilled from French models, create its distinct personality.

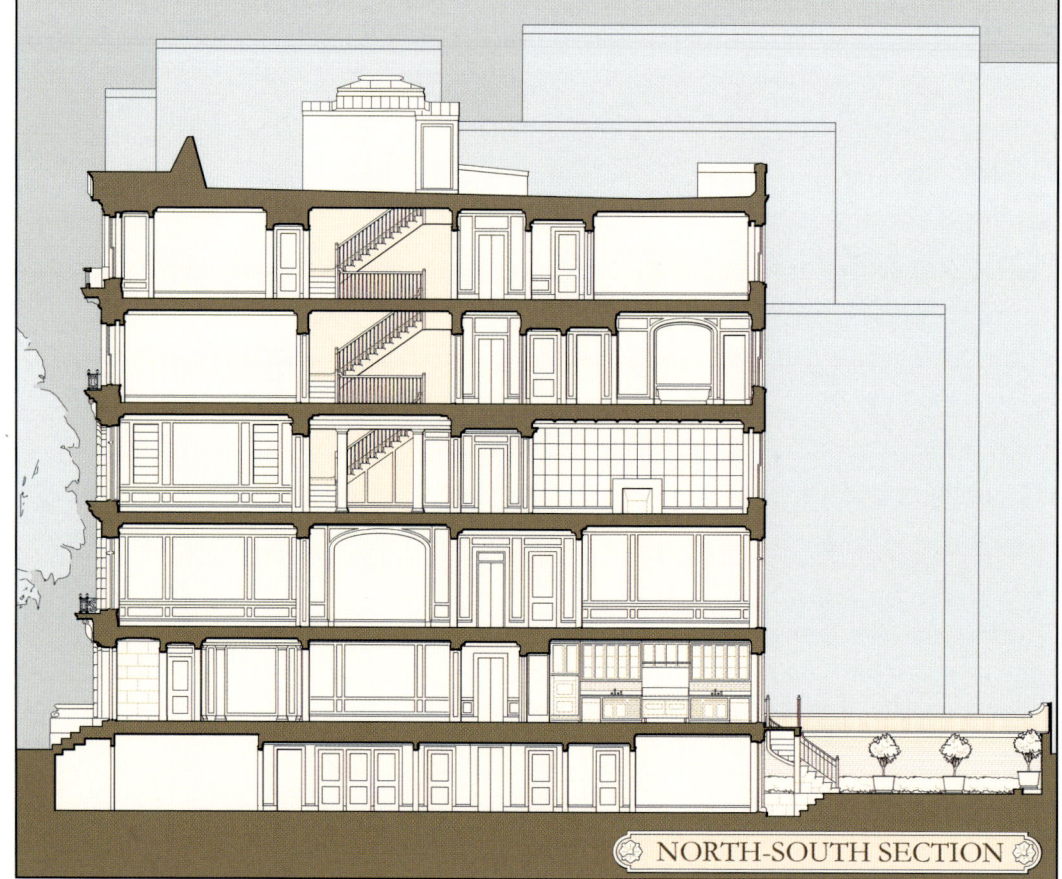

NORTH-SOUTH SECTION

likely would have existed in the original house. PPA softened the details to design rooms more appropriate for everyday living. For example, the ground-floor kitchen, carried out in ebonized wood, with rough-hewn herringbone floors, built-in antique French cabinetry, and large fireplace inset with a pizza oven, has the ambiance of a country kitchen. On the piano nobile, paint-finished paneling in the south parlor and mahogany paneling in the dining room set off antique mantels from France. In the third-floor library, PPA tempered the elaborate French Baroque window—the central feature of the facade—with walls of reclaimed knotty pine—a gesture that creates a bold contrast. The pivot of the design, however, is the oval stair that gracefully spirals between the two levels of public rooms through the core of the house. A grand, almost decadent, nod to the Beaux-Arts idiom, this is the moment where the spirited French character of the design is unleashed. A more modest orthogonal stair signals the transition between public and private spaces and leads from the third floor to the two levels of bedrooms on the upper stories.

This project also incorporated new methods of construction that are virtually indistinguishable from what could have been accomplished by skilled craftsmen. Both the marble-clad steel superstructure of the stair and water-jet-cut steel and bronze handrail are products of robotically generated manufacturing. Executed by computer numeric control methods in Portland, Oregon, the stair was shipped to New York and set into place.

ABOVE

With Flemish bond brickwork, stone band courses, and a bifurcated stair connecting the kitchen to the garden, the new north facade is a modern counterpoint to the street facade.

OPPOSITE

The elliptical sweep of the stair and its steel and bronze handrail was realized through digital production.

RIGHT

The spirited French appeal of the design is reflected in the stair, which spirals between the first and third floors of the house.

BEAUX-ARTS TOWNHOUSE ✤ 77

LEFT
Lacquered paneling in the living room sets a tone of French formality.

OPPOSITE
The kitchen is centered on an asymmetrical limestone hearth—complete with pizza oven— that anchors the paneled breakfast area.

BELOW
Salvaged pine beams were milled into paneling for the library, creating a bold juxtaposition with the room's elaborate baroque window, the central feature of the street facade.

LENOX HILL TOWNHOUSE

WHEN PPA BEGAN WORK ON THIS LENOX HILL townhouse, it was vacant and unfinished, a brick skeleton behind a delicately carved but downtrodden landmarked limestone facade. The house exemplifies the early-twentieth-century trend of architects transforming the monotonous stretches of high-stooped brownstones on New York's Upper East Side by expanding and reclothing the facades, removing stoops, and reorienting the layouts. Developer George McCollom built this townhouse as one of nine Italianate row houses in 1872; however, it was converted into a classically inspired house with an entrance at street level in 1917, when Carl Schoen commissioned Henry Pelton to design a new elegantly understated French neoclassical facade and reconfigure the interiors. When the 10,000-square-foot house switched hands to its current owners after a series of incomplete renovations, it was a shell.

PPA rejuvenated the neglected street facade, its historic details, and ironwork, and designed a new areaway, ironwork railing, and gate at pedestrian level in keeping with the building's historic fabric. However, the project's main challenges lay in creating a seamless transition between the historic facade and the new interiors, as well as designing an appropriate and livable family home in such a large and vertically defined space. The seven-story, nineteen-foot-wide house encompasses a two-story penthouse added by Pelton in 1917 and also includes two sublevels. In these interior spaces, PPA struck a fine balance between a restrained classical approach and the stripped modernist aesthetic that the clients admired. Unlike the highly eclectic interiors incorporating many different stylistic inspirations that would have originally existed in the house, the firm designed the rooms to reflect the level of detail and distillation in the simple, yet elegantly appointed, exterior elevation. While the architecture is consistent throughout, it becomes increasingly light and more abstract as the rooms rise through the house. Picking up the character and materials of the facade, PPA carried the stone into the vestibule and intimately scaled entry hall. At the center of the house, a dramatic oval stair ascends a full five stories, lit from above through structural glass block on an upper terrace. To temper the formal layout of the plan and the center stair, PPA carved sitting areas out of landings through the core of the building, creating comfortable, cozy, and

OPPOSITE
Polished wood floors in the first-floor stair hall contrast with the limestone foyer beyond while distilled classical details unify the entire entry with a crisp and modern expression.

BELOW
A new areaway with ironwork based on the historic fabric of the house frames the restored facade.

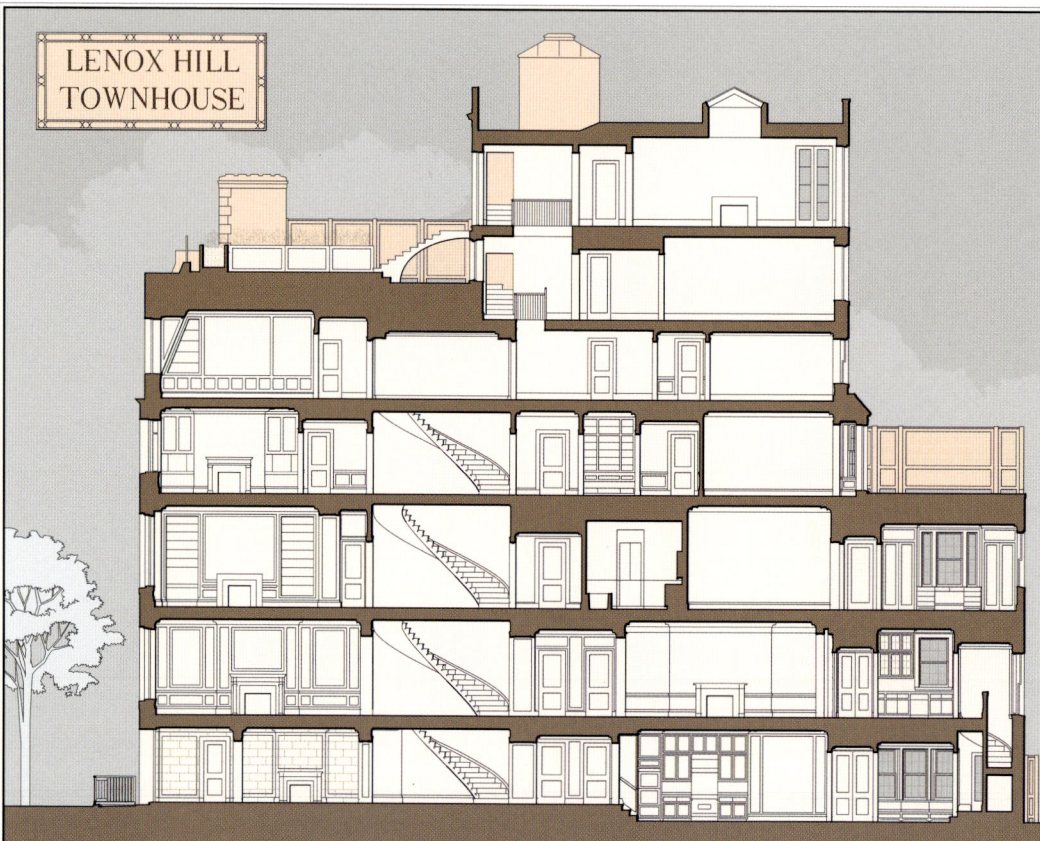

ABOVE

The second-floor stair landing was reinvented as a book-lined sitting area between the living and dining rooms.

SECTION

The two-story penthouse is expressed as a modern addition, breaking with the more traditional architecture of the lower floors.

OPPOSITE

The elliptical stair spirals up to the fifth floor and is lit from above through structural glass on the north terrace.

livable spaces. A bay in the playroom in what was the old servants' hall to the rear was transformed into a warm and inviting nook to congregate. The public rooms on the lower levels—including the plaster-finished living room, the chocolate-colored dining room finished in polished Venetian plaster, and the stained mahogany-paneled library—are more conservatively established. But, rather than maintaining them as separate and distinct spaces, pocket doors slide back to reveal the full depth of the building, creating a transparency throughout and making the house more open, family friendly, and well-suited for entertaining. To emphasize the accumulative nature of the house's architecture, PPA expressed the two later penthouse levels as a modernist addition. Here, a complete break is made with the lower stories and a new steel-and-wood stair slides behind the penthouse facade and leads from an exercise room on the sixth floor up to a sleek classically proportioned music room lit by a skylight and French doors on three sides. Throughout, Victoria Hagan's decoration of neutral colors and simple profiles echoes the essence of the architecture, infusing the interiors with light, air, and a relaxed atmosphere appropriate to a large young family.

This project also involved the creation of outdoor spaces, including a small rear yard and a lattice-framed north terrace accessed from the upper level of the penthouse by a sweeping stair. In the spirit of A. J. Davis, the northern penthouse facade is embellished with recessed spandrels decorated with a Greek key motif. Its balanced simplicity masks the complexity of the multilevel room configuration, multiple terrace doors, and penthouse stair.

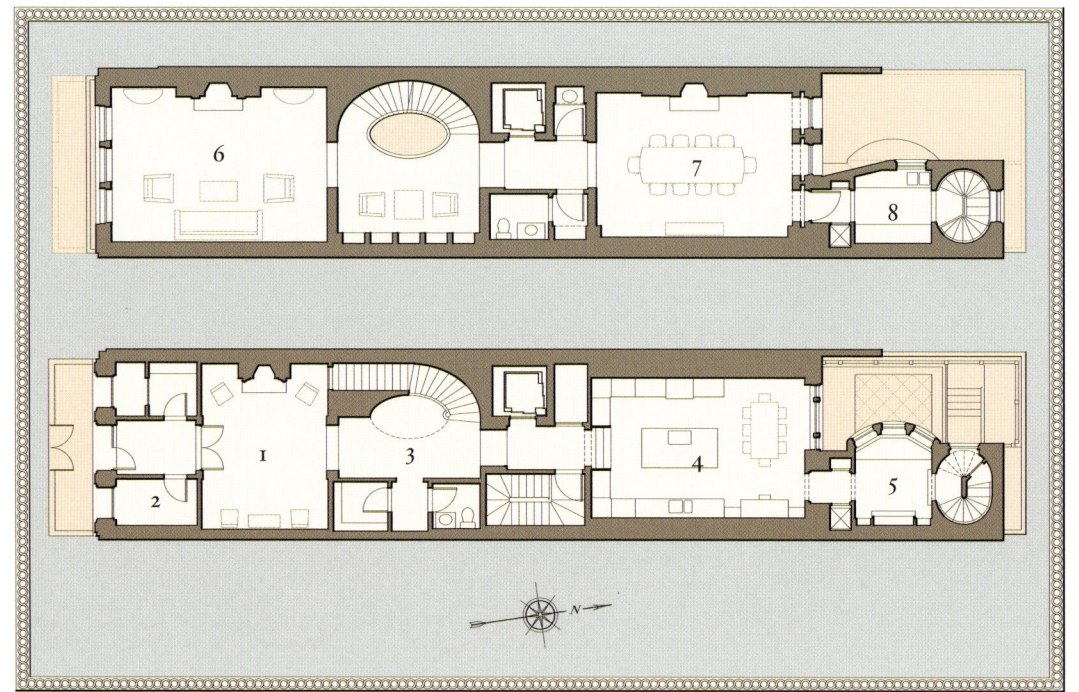

PLAN

A lozenge-shaped stair at the back of the plan connects the first-floor kitchen and rear sitting room to the pantry above.

1. Entry hall
2. Mudroom
3. Stair hall
4. Kitchen
5. Playroom
6. Living room
7. Dining room
8. Butler's pantry

OPPOSITE

The plaster-paneled living room is centered on a classical chimneypiece.

BELOW

The limestone entry hall bridges the architecture of the exterior and interior by incorporating the same material used on the facade.

OPPOSITE TOP

A mirrored door leading to the butler's pantry mimics the windows and balances the dining room.

OPPOSITE BOTTOM

The subdued and dark tones of the furniture and the mahogany paneling create a formal yet cozy library on the third floor.

RIGHT

The ground-floor kitchen, set on axis with the front door, steps down from the stair hall.

BELOW

The kitchen faces south over the small rear garden.

RIGHT
The penthouse facade stoop connects the music room to the north terrace.

BELOW
A minimalist black and white music room occupies the top floor of the house and is set with tall, paired doors.

OPPOSITE
A steel and wood stair slides past the windows of the addition while another short run of steps leads to the north terrace.

LIMESTONE MANSION

BELOW
Herbert Lucas's classical facade from the 1910s is capped by a new mansard by Swanke Hayden Connell Architects.

OPPOSITE
An iron laylight enhances the domed ceiling of the main stair.

Located in one of the Upper East Side's best-preserved stretches of turn-of-the-century mansions, this landmarked limestone and marble house was originally commissioned in 1899 by grocery magnate James E. Nichols in the Beaux-Arts style and designed by the fashionable C. P. H. Gilbert, whose Fifth Avenue houses and chateaux have come to embody the extravagance of the Gilded Age. As a reflection of changing tastes, in the 1910s Herbert Lucas—an architect who later designed the Savoy Plaza while working at McKim, Mead & White—pared down and classicized Gilbert's asymmetrical, baroque entrance facade that had a door to the east, framed by ornately carved columns and bull's-eyes, and a bowed three-story bay to the west. At that time, the penthouse—housed in Gilbert's hipped roof, punched with carved round-arched dormers—was reconfigured, expanding the roofline of the building.

During the span of this project, the exterior was restored and a new mansard roof put on the house. PPA, as associated architect, was responsible for re-establishing the interior architecture of the six-story, 18,000-square-foot building in what was one of the most substantial residential commissions in Manhattan in recent years. What had initially begun as a consultant role in the project turned into a larger opportunity to impact the direction and tone of the interiors. The major challenge rested in reconciling a new design with the plans already prepared by the executive architect and with Gilbert's original work, much of which consisted of standardized off-the-shelf elements and moldings.

The formal and distinctive street facade set the tone for a succession of Beaux-Arts–style wood and plaster-paneled interiors with extensive stonework. Given the prominence and opulence of the thirty-five-foot-wide townhouse, PPA rose to the challenge of devising a program of interior architecture that presented, in distilled and abstracted form, the sensuality and abundance of New York's eclectic period at the turn of the twentieth century. A new entrance hall, modeled from the same type of limestone as the Frick Collection, south on Fifth Avenue, is resplendent with paired Doric pilasters, marble floors, and a broad double door and transom embellished with new ironwork inspired by the details of the existing original front door. The wide, rectangular, plaster-paneled stair wrought with ironwork and a mahogany handrail, extending between the first and fourth floors, underscores the

generous proportions of the house. The stair culminates under a vaulted ceiling and large, radiating, circular laylight on the fourth floor, where a gallery created by a pattern of overlaid pilasters, intricately carved capitals—adapted from the drawings of Percier and Fontaine—and arched pediments formalize the space.

Similarly, the grand entertaining rooms on the lower floors reflect the Beaux-Arts origins of the house. With windows and curved bays along an areaway to the west—a feature held over from Gilbert's original design—the public rooms on the second and third floors have gently bowed walls and two exposures—a rare feature, for in most New York City townhouses the exposure is limited to the front and rear. PPA expressed the second-floor stair hall and landing, lit by three tall windows, as a comfortable sitting area embellished by a rhythm of pilasters and delicately detailed Corinthian capitals, whose light-feathering acanthus leaves were inspired by the work of the Danish master C. F. Hansen. The landing connects the living room at the front of the house, embellished with vertical acanthus plaster panels, to the dining room to the rear, where a new mantel, befittingly inspired by one at Le Petit Trianon, centers the grand space. While the architecture of the third-floor oak-paneled library is more restrained, its carved ceiling, an element original to the house, and dark marble fireplace capture the exuberance of the Beaux-Arts style. A family dining room and kitchen, separate from the large basement kitchen for catering, rounds out the floor. Above the fourth-floor master suite, a more intimately scaled stair leads to two additional floors of bedrooms. Decorated by Shaun Jackson, these multilayered interiors fluidly and appropriately express the architecture of this important townhouse and properly set off the client's art collection.

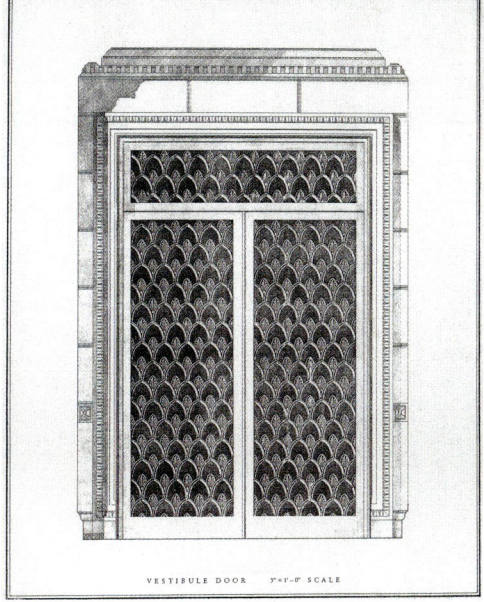

TOP AND ABOVE

The original front door inspired new ironwork for the interior vestibule door.

ABOVE LEFT

The west-facing marble entrance hall with terrace doors reflects the full-bodied classical expression of the interiors.

OPPOSITE

Metalworker Jean Wiart carried out the stair rail's pattern of rosettes and decorative leaves.

ABOVE

The design for the balustrade rosette.

OPPOSITE TOP

The west-facing curved wall in the living room is articulated by the sweep of the denticulated cornice.

OPPOSITE BOTTOM

The antique marble mantel inspired the scrolling plaster panels in the living room.

RIGHT AND BELOW

The fluted pilasters and capitals in the stair hall were inspired by the work of C. F. Hansen.

ABOVE

A mantel based on an example from Le Petit Trianon anchors the dining room.

LEFT

Mahogany double doors open from the second floor stair hall into the dining room, where architectural moldings frame wallpaper panels.

OPPOSITE

A bedroom entrance is framed by bookcases and set on axis with a mantel carved with Adamesque detail.

ABOVE
The marble library mantel is carved with acanthus leaves.

RIGHT
The oak paneling in the library is set between shallow pilasters that frame the window and door openings.

UPPER EAST SIDE TOWNHOUSE

ONE OF FOUR BROWNSTONES DESIGNED BY WILLIAM MCNAMARA in 1872 for developer William McEvily, this five-story Italianate townhouse stands as a vestige of the block's once-unified street wall created by strips of brownstones constructed during the speculative building boom of the second half of the nineteenth century. While several similar brownstones remain on the block, this street—one of the most charming in Manhattan's Upper East Side Historic District—was transformed in the early years of the twentieth century at the hands of such talents as C. P. H. Gilbert, Delano & Aldrich, and Walker & Hazard with an assortment of Beaux-Arts mansions, smaller Federal Revival houses, and carriage houses. Although this house retained its stoop, unlike many of its variety, much of the embellishment on the brownstone facade had been lost. For the client, a couple with young children, PPA returned this nineteen-foot-wide house—which had been divided into apartments—to a single-family home and reestablished its architectural identity within the historic streetscape, entirely rebuilding the 7,500-square-foot structure behind the restored street facade.

The adjacent house, at one time occupied by architect James Gamble Rogers, was the best preserved among the four original brownstones; its example, accompanied by archival photographs, created a template to follow in bringing back the facade's stripped details, including all of the window enframements, the pedimented entry portico supported by Tuscan columns, and the cast iron stair rail. In addition to restoring the original modillioned cornice, PPA designed a new front door and cast-iron newel posts, balusters, and hand railings for the stoop and areaway to recapture their original expression. Skilled craftsman carried out the exterior's extensive sandstone-plaster restoration, fashioning the carved detail by hand over an armature of embedded stainless steel. In the rear, PPA removed a two-story addition and extended the plane of the facade to the thirty-foot rear-yard limit, opening up the garden to its full width. The new understated brick and limestone facade evokes the spirit of the neighboring garden elevations.

Typically, brownstones are characterized by their offset stoop and front entrance, which connect to a straight stair that ascends against a party wall. In redesigning the interior, PPA relocated the stair to the middle of the building, a compositional break that

OPPOSITE
The new vestibule door based on neighboring examples reflects the soaring 11 ½ foot ceiling height of the parlor floor.

BELOW
A newly designed front door, cast iron newel posts, balusters, and hand railings recapture the house's original expression.

ABOVE

Traditional steel French doors in the living room create an abstracted Palladian window that opens out to juliet balconies.

ABOVE RIGHT

The removal of a slender rear addition renovated in the 1970s allowed the garden, designed by Madison Cox, to be opened to its full width.

reorients the plan around the core of the house and creates an aesthetic surprise inside. On the parlor level, PPA designed an elegant enfilade of arches—reinforced by the unusually high ceiling—that carries from the north sitting room through a semielliptical stair hall to the living room in the rear. In the central stair hall, a Palladian archway with faux-grained Ionic columns embraces the stair. A garden entrance, tucked underneath the stoop, enters into a painted wood-paneled family room that leads through to a warm paneled kitchen with a *verre eglomisé* (gilded glass) backsplash, conceived by Thomas Jayne, and back to the dining room, where steel-sashed doors open out into Madison Cox's granite-paved garden. PPA emphasized the interconnectedness of the spaces. For example, the kitchen opens into the dining room and a bull's-eye window in the stair looks onto the family room; on the parlor level, arched pocket doors slide back to reveal the depth of the house. And in the spirit of old New York, the warm hues of the wainscoting and trim, all in dark oak, evoke the intimacy of a nineteenth-century Italianate house. Throughout, the well-proportioned rooms come alive with the multilayered color of Jeffrey Bilhuber's decoration. PPA located the master suite and an oak-paneled library on the third floor, and placed children's bedrooms on the fourth floor. The design culminates in the fifth-floor stair landing—or family room—distinguished by a sail vault, circular oculus, and built-in shelving. The landing connects to a guest suite, exercise room, and stair leading up to a rooftop garden.

ABOVE

Through historical research, the facade's stripped brownstone details were brought back.

BELOW

A Palladian archway articulated in dark oak expresses the stair on the parlor level.

ABOVE

On the parlor floor, an enfilade of arches extends through the public rooms and is anchored by the arched window in the living room.

OPPOSITE

The kitchen, with oak-and-sycamore cabinetry and *verre eglomisé* (gilded glass) backsplash, connects to the dining room.

RIGHT

A screen of fluted Doric columns introduces the dark oak stair on the kitchen level.

FAR RIGHT

A glimpse of the family room is captured through a bull's-eye window on the stair landing.

BELOW

In the family room, bookshelves are built into the window casings, which overlook the areaway.

UPPER EAST SIDE TOWNHOUSE ❖ 105

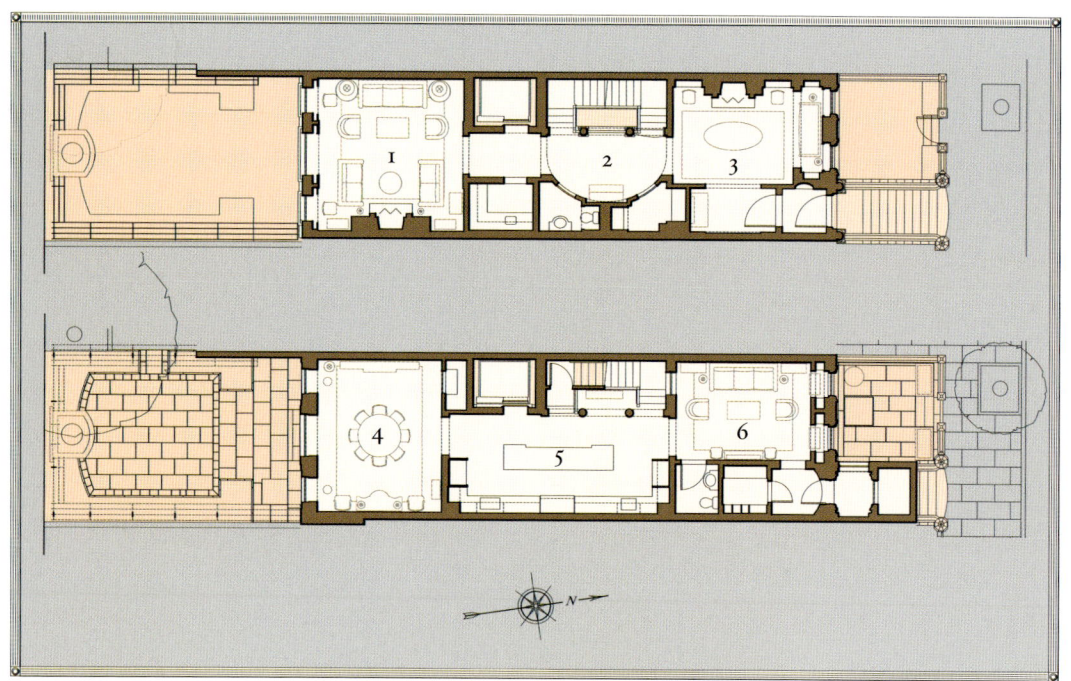

PLAN

The plan was reoriented around the central stair with a variety of rooms receiving light from the top-floor skylight.

1. Living room
2. Stair hall
3. Sitting room
4. Dining room
5. Kitchen
6. Family room

OPPOSITE

The house culminates in the fifth-floor family room, lit by an oculus at the center of a sail vault.

BELOW LEFT

Thin stiles and rails create the framework for the broad panels of grasscloth in an upstairs bedroom.

BELOW

The library is paneled in dark oak and has a Tudor-inspired decorative ceiling.

GROSVENOR ATTERBURY TOWNHOUSE

OPPOSITE

The grand stair curves up from the elegant black and white marble floor of the entrance hall, which connects back to the kitchen and garden beyond.

BELOW

The delicate ironwork pattern of the front door was modeled after Atterbury's original designs.

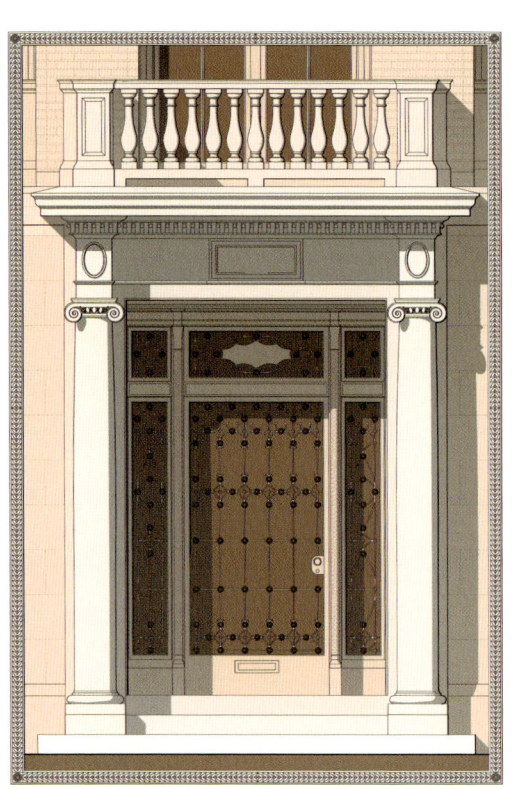

One of the most influential architects, town planners, and inventors of the first half of the twentieth century, Grosvenor Atterbury was best known for the design of Forest Hills Gardens, a model suburb in Queens for the Russell Sage Foundation, and for an array of site-specific, naturalistic country houses, primarily on Long Island. A native New Yorker, Atterbury also built a substantial practice in the city and designed a number of townhouses, including this house from 1915, commissioned by prominent insurance executive Edwin Cornell Jameson and his wife, Mary Gardner Jameson. More inclined to work in vernacular or medieval styles using a painterly palette of materials and picturesque massing, Atterbury was slightly less comfortable working in the Colonial Revival mode, having been formed as a designer before the classical revival had fully permeated American architecture. At heart, he was a designer of model tenements and town plans and was at his best in projects that addressed issues of planning and cost-effectiveness.

The plan of this twenty-eight-foot-wide, six-story townhouse reveals Atterbury's strength as an architect. During the course of the project, PPA completely reconstructed the building, which had been modified into offices in 1953, and restored it to a single-family dwelling. PPA sought both to respect and improve upon Atterbury's original design. Outside, the firm restored the landmarked street facade of red brick and snow-white Yule marble and replaced the stones that had been effectively melted by New York's harsh climate. In rebuilding the rear facade, the firm matched Atterbury's original white glazed brick—a hygienic and cost-saving measure carried over from his tenement work. On the roof, PPA expanded the bulkhead into a penthouse loggia, designed to be invisible from the street, which fronts onto a terrace with an outdoor fireplace.

Atterbury's comingling of Colonial Revival and French influences is more typical of the casual eclecticism of the 1890s than the scholarly classicism of the 1910s, when the house was actually built. On the ground floor, where Atterbury deftly provided a separate service door and a full-width foyer, the entrance sequence remains much as the architect left it. Meanwhile, to better articulate the interior architecture, PPA refined aspects of other spaces and rooms—subsequently decorated by Christie Hansen—in the spirit of Atterbury, using his

OPPOSITE

Bronze doors and sidelights connect the full-width entrance hall to the vestibule on the street.

LEFT

Three pairs of bronze doors open from the penthouse loggia to the terrace.

BELOW

The blue walls of the powder room are accented with delicately carved plaster garlands and figural groups inspired by Atterbury's moldings.

original design as a springboard. On the piano nobile, the architect had united the reception room with an elegant, symmetrical enfilade that masked the presence of a butler's pantry, discretely tucked into the rear yard, and organized the space around an ample well-crafted Colonial Revival stair that rises dramatically the full height of the house. On the second-floor landing—a music room centered on a fireplace—PPA opened up the ceiling considerably by removing a large artificially lit laylight and accommodated the height deficit by designing new pedestals for Atterbury's pilasters. In restoring the three arched French doors in the formal living room, PPA reopened the transom lights (which had been blocked in a previous renovation), an improvement that draws more light into the room and highlights new strié painted plaster finishes and the antique fireplace. In the rear, the firm replaced the formerly low and broad opening leading into Atterbury's oval dining room with a fluid semielliptical vault. In the dining room, newly opened vistas to a windowed alcove and a top-lit servery create more natural light, while the space is given elegant expression by a gold-leaf ceiling, new plaster grilles to disguise the air conditioning vents, and a fireplace designed especially to meet the curves of the room.

While the third floor contains a library and guest rooms, the upper levels of the house are devoted to the clients' private quarters: the master suite, children's bedrooms, a playroom, and a family room. An upshot of his interest in ventilation, particularly in low income housing, Atterbury's manner of drawing light and air into the upper floors is perhaps the most interesting element of his original design. By extending a light shaft through the core of the building above the second floor, he enabled all of the bathrooms, dressing rooms, and stair halls to benefit from windows—a strategy he frequently used in his townhouse designs. The clients have assigned the light well (which PPA extended above the third floor) another use, transforming it into a climbing wall for their children.

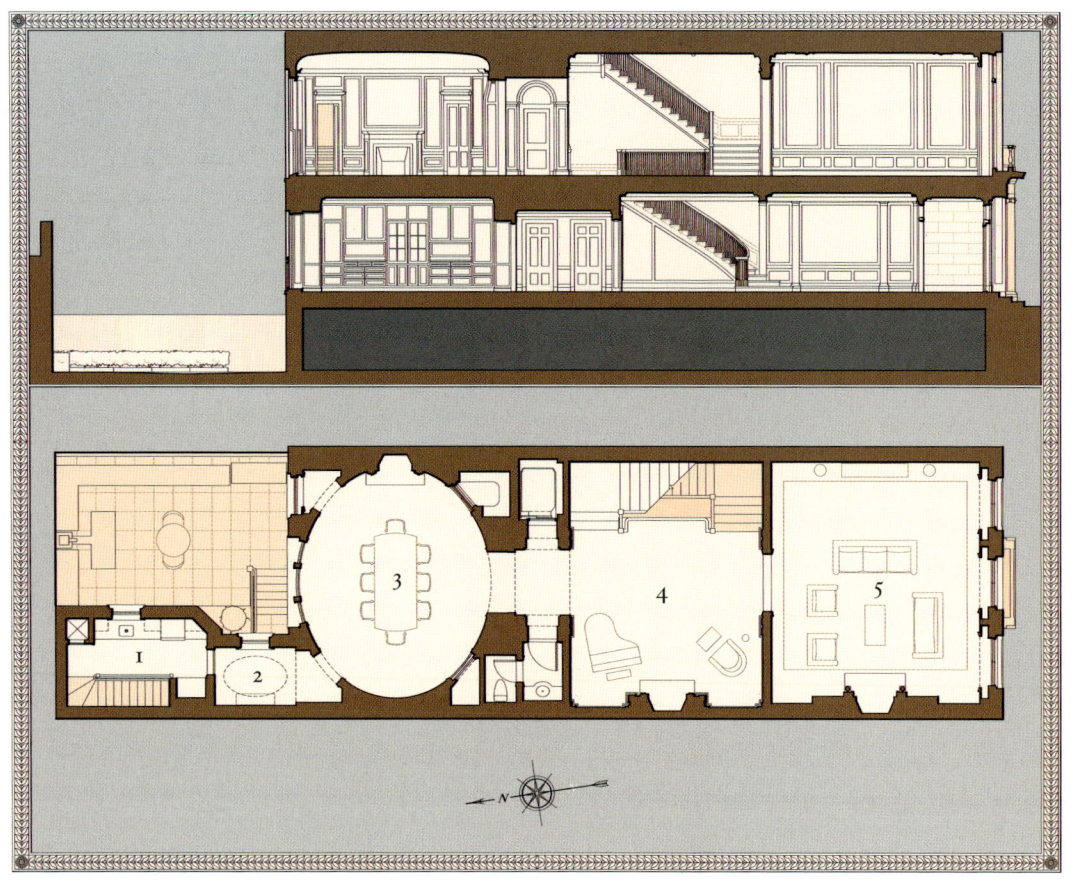

PLAN AND SECTION

From the entrance hall, the stair leads up to the piano nobile, where the music room connects the living room and elliptical dining room.

1. Pantry
2. Servery
3. Dining room
4. Music room
5. Living room

OPPOSITE

The second-floor landing is transformed into a music room enhanced by fluted pilasters and paneled wainscoting.

BELOW

Plaster paneling, a decorative ceiling, arched window frames, and an antique mantel formalize the south-facing living room.

LEFT

The dining room is anchored by a hand-carved white-marble mantel especially designed to meet the curves of the space.

OPPOSITE BOTTOM

The formerly low and broad opening into the dining room was transformed into a fluid semielliptical vault.

BELOW

Newly opened window views light the gold-leafed ceiling in the dining room. Plaster anthemion grilles of palmettes and lotus blossoms incorporated into the elliptical walls mask air conditioning vents.

ABOVE

Atterbury's light well is transformed into a climbing wall.

RIGHT

The top-floor landing, lit by a rectangular laylight and bull's-eye window, leads to the penthouse loggia and terrace.

OPPOSITE TOP LEFT

Curved walls and an alcove add character to a bedroom vestibule.

OPPOSITE TOP RIGHT

An arched bronze French door, inspired by Atterbury's original window designs, opens from the family room onto a hedge-lined terrace.

OPPOSITE BOTTOM

A large kitchen with ash-veneer cabinetry overlooks the rear garden and connects to a staff pantry.

SAN FRANCISCO HOUSE

Perched high above San Francisco Bay, this Mediterranean-style stucco house in Seacliff, built in 1928, represents the neighborhood's golden age when houses and estates sprang up along the area's distinctive cliffs, in a district of the city that was once occupied by a large military reservation. With panoramic views stretching from the Golden Gate Bridge to the Marin Headlands, this house possesses unobstructed vistas north but is open to the street and nestled closely among its neighbors. For the most part, the exterior and facades of the house, embellished with baroque details, withstood the hand of time; inside, however, the house had been stripped and only the rustic-beam ceilings, tiles on the risers and treads of the stairs, and a pair of heavy wooden doors had survived. In renovating this 6,000-square-foot house for a family, PPA reimagined the house's historic architecture to emphasize its fundamentally simple, Spanish-inspired character, an approach that enabled the design to envelope the immaterial qualities of the site, such as air, light, and views that flood the interiors. At the same time, it allowed for the decoration by Katie Ridder and the gardens by Madison Cox to vividly emerge.

By screening the front of the house, PPA created a discreet enclosure. Here the firm designed a new wrought-iron gate and thick stucco garden wall in the Spanish idiom to produce a sense of privacy. The front door of the U-shaped house is buried in the middle of the site. Madison Cox's room-like terrace and his small garden, planted with boxwood and palm trees, create an intimate entrance sequence that steps down from the street. To the north, where the house opens to three levels, Cox's more formal French-inspired parterre creates a tiny oasis within the lot's enclosure where colors pop against the expanse of the blue horizon.

With few moldings or overtly classical details, PPA distilled the interior architecture almost to the point of oversimplification, which allowed for the virtues of the rooms' lofty proportions and the texture of the thick plaster walls—so associated with the Spanish style—to stand out. By finessing the house's boxy plan, the firm was able to modernize and interrelate the various rooms. A vaulted entrance hall, lit from the east by arched French doors, is a sundrenched meditative spot that overlooks the front garden and runs alongside the

OPPOSITE

White walls set off the tiled stair, balustrade, and a coffered ceiling composed of antique and new panels.

ABOVE

A walkway lined with boxwood leads to the inner courtyard and front entrance of the house.

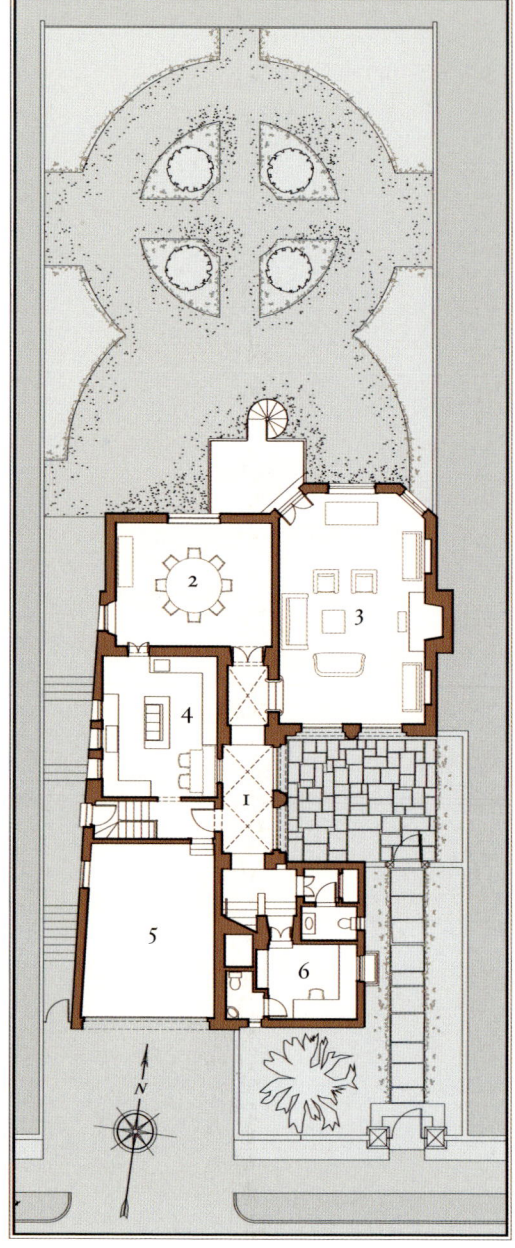

PLAN

The U-shaped house is centered on an intimate roomlike garden terrace and opens to a parterre to the north facing San Francisco Bay.

1. Entry hall
2. Dining room
3. Living room
4. Kitchen
5. Garage
6. Office

LEFT

The sunlit vaulted entry hall overlooks the front garden and connects to the dining room.

kitchen. Here the firm added a bull's-eye window to create a dialogue between the two previously unlinked spaces. Throughout the public rooms, walls were rendered in natural plaster and painted a uniform whitewash, creating a stark enveloping background that was then used as a springboard for decorator Katie Ridder's program, which incorporates bright colors and is expressed frankly as ornament, highlighting a variety of artistic elements. In the dining room, for example, bas-relief of flamingos, deer, and serpents—inspired by the amphibious work of Chagall and carried out in collaboration with the San Francisco sculptor Paul Lanier—adorn the walls. Stencils on the beamed ceiling in both the dining and living room accentuate the house's historic fabric with a touch of whimsy. More baroque in spirit are the bright colors of the applied models of California flowers on the green walls of the powder room and the panels of red leather tile secured with bronze studs in the basement media room. Upstairs, an ornate nineteenth-century panel that Pennoyer bought at auction was incorporated into the design of the second-floor hallway alongside two additional panels that were commissioned as complements.

ABOVE

The stenciled beams of the living-room ceiling evoke the house's Spanish character.

OVERLEAF

The living room is anchored by an *en trumeau* French chimneypiece discovered in Paris by the architect.

OPPOSITE TOP
Paul Lanier's bas-relief of flamingos, deer, and serpents adorn the thick plaster walls of the dining room.

OPPOSITE BOTTOM
In the kitchen, dark wood cabinetry contrasts with the blue tiled walls.

RIGHT
The basement media room is paneled in red leather floor tiles secured with bronze studs.

BELOW
The attic sitting room opens north to views of San Francisco Bay.

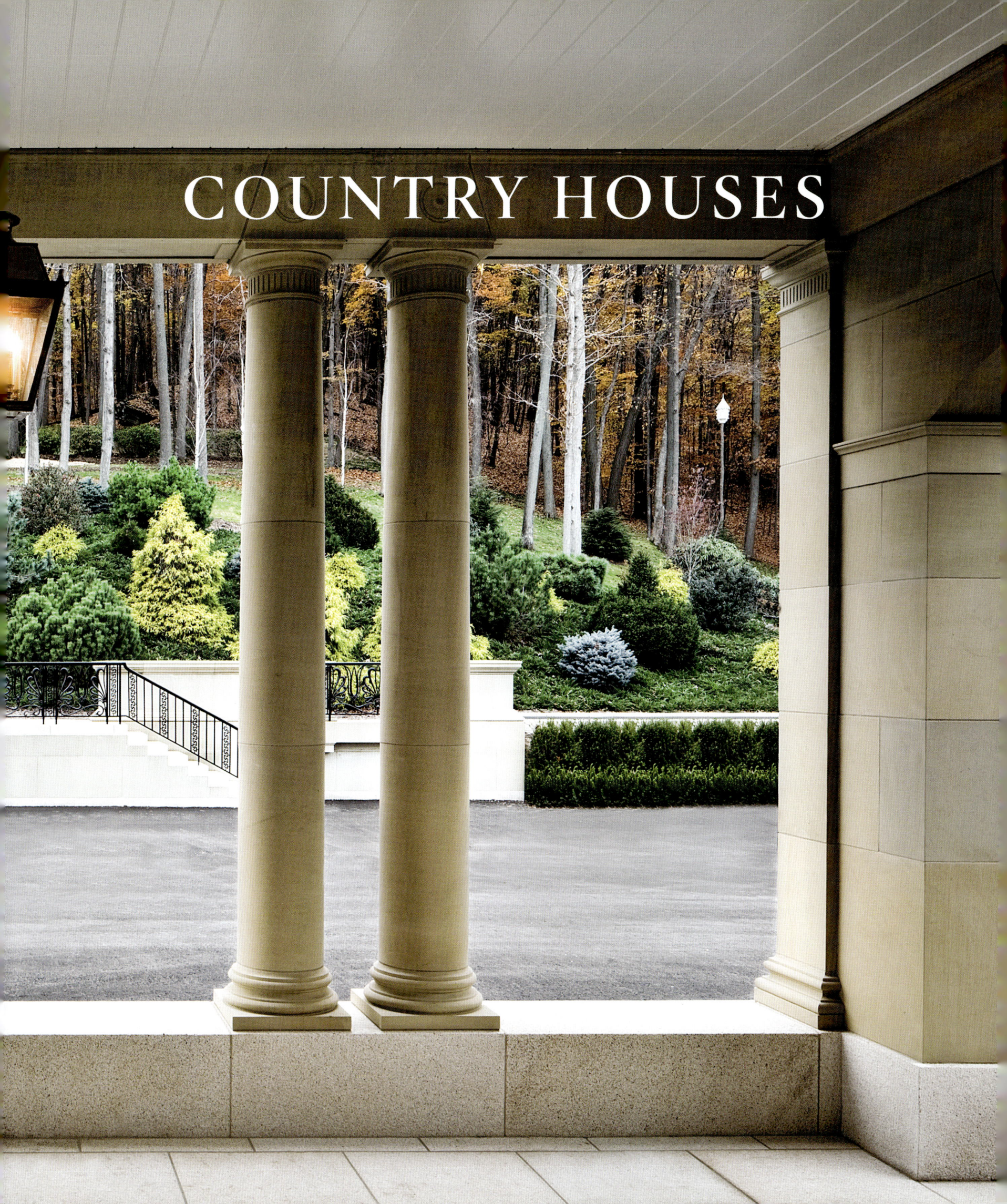
COUNTRY HOUSES

ADIRONDACK CAMP

For the design of this camp, located deep in a wooded preserve once part of William Rockefeller's 27,000-acre property in New York's Adirondack Park, PPA looked to the longstanding tradition of the Great Camps. In the late nineteenth century, the networks of lakes and the seclusion of the Adirondacks' wilderness grew in popularity as a seasonal draw, particularly among the so-called captains of industry. What began as modest camps grew into self-sufficient compounds of rustic luxury set amid extensive acreage in remote locations. William West Durant, son of a railroad tycoon, developed his family's land holdings in the area with what were the first of the Great Camps—Camp Pine Knot, sold to Collis P. Huntington; Camp Uncas, sold to J. P Morgan; and Sagamore, sold to Alfred G. Vanderbilt—setting an architectural standard that combined elements of the Arts and Crafts and Swiss Chalet styles. Some were constructed by local builders while others were designed by some of the most astute architects of the era, but they all display a comparable level of self-conscious rusticity masking the creature comforts within. While the programs of these complexes were quite complicated, the use of natural and native materials, such as logs and local stone, combined with shingled overhangs, porches, and simple proportions gave rise to a distinctive vernacular that has come to be known as the Adirondack style.

With a comprehensive understanding of the area's architectural tradition, PPA embarked on a design that evoked the characteristic modesty and rustic reserve of the area's lodges, drawing inspiration from Robert H. Robertson's 1908 scheme for Camp Santanoni, Robert Pruyn's preserve on Newcomb Lake. Inspired by the architecture of Norway and North Russia, Robertson offset the black-stained peeled-log facades of Camp Santanoni with bright red door and window frames. For this project, PPA also chose to stain the shiplap cedar boards of the facades black and used red trim—a trademark of the Adirondack style—to allow the house to project against the shadowy wooded surroundings. Here the texture and color of the native materials—the stained cedar, timber, and stone—create a dynamic rhythm as the house bends with the contours of the site. Porches of white pine run the width of the house, creating an outdoor refuge in which to experience the lakeside views.

ABOVE

Dormers create clerestory light in the living room and frame the monumental fireplace at the east end.

OPPOSITE

The living room fireplace, constructed by a local mason with uncut, hand-selected stones, lines up with the architrave of the wood paneling inspired by Bernard Maybeck.

PLAN

The butterfly plan amplifies light and views of the lake.

1. Garage
2. Mudroom
3. Kitchen
4. Screened porch
5. Dining room
6. Living room
7. Guest wing hall
8. Guest bedroom
9. Guest sitting room

BELOW

A porch of white pine with peeled-log columns extends the width of the house.

OPPOSITE

The stair, embellished with a peeled-log balustrade, incorporates jute, a traditional method of caulking, and boards reclaimed from derelict local barns.

OVERLEAF

The red trim, inspired by Camp Santanoni, allows the house to stand out against its wooded surroundings.

Inside, PPA wove natural materials into the design, allowing their virtues to create a decorative effect. The Great Camps, often complexes of smaller buildings attached by porches, revolve around a large gathering spot—or main lodge—with a central fireplace. In keeping with this custom, the firm located the vaulted cedar-lined living room, lit by upper-level dormers, at the center of the plan and anchored the space around a monumental fieldstone fireplace; a chandelier of interwoven antlers hangs at the center. The main staircase, articulated in peeled logs, natural branches, and different species of wood, relies on the inherent colors of the materials for texture and interest. Throughout the rooms—decorated by Ann O'Leary—the firm used finishes of cedar, beaded board, and painted wood to exude a simple rusticity and, at either end of the house, angled screened porches and guest rooms toward the lake to take in the quiet scenery of the untouched landscape.

Straddling the long driveway that meanders through the woods, the long barn marks the entrance to the house; its arched tunnel creates a sense of arrival to the compound and offers a feeling of boundary and welcomed enclosure in the face of the wild and remote surroundings. It contains a large bunkroom for visiting children and separate staff quarters, both rustically finished with new and reused cedar panels and timber. On the lower level, five bays—some of which have openings on both sides of the building—house a collection of vintage World War II trucks, jeeps, and all-terrain vehicles for navigating the vast network of trails carved into the extensive acreage of the preserve's shared land.

OPPOSITE

The open dining room and living room occupy the center of the plan and create a central gathering spot in the tradition of the Adirondack Great Camp.

LEFT

The glass windows in the heated porch, which can be replaced with screens in the summer, frame views of the lake.

BELOW

The lantern at the long barn's entrance was reclaimed from the original Rockefeller railroad station on the preserve.

HOUSE ON PENOBSCOT BAY

OPPOSITE

Oiled and waxed oak paneling and a beamed ceiling, nautical in spirit, enhances the double-height stair hall.

BELOW

Paneled piers frame the entrance into the stair hall and reinforce the inviting enfilade extending from the living room to the breakfast room beyond.

THIS GENTLY RAMBLING SHINGLE STYLE HOUSE, SET ON THE edge of a fifty-acre site on an island off the coast of Maine was designed to graciously perch at the crest of a narrow ridge overlooking the thoroughfare between Penobscot Bay and the open Atlantic Ocean. Historically, the livelihood of this remote island centered on farming and fishing. From the early nineteenth century to the 1930s, a herd of sheep had grazed the farmland and meadow comprising this property. At the turn of the twentieth century, the rusticators, summer people from Boston and New York, descended on the island, drawn by the stunning natural landscape and rugged beauty; they shared a respect for its traditions and weathered architecture, purchasing or building houses suitable to the seaside setting. PPA looked to the vernacular in the design for this summer home for a family with young children. The house is utterly simple in its outward guise; carried out in an almost severe Shingle Style endemic to the island, it follows the example set by such Boston architects and firms as H. Daland Chandler, William Y. Peters, and Wheelwright & Haven, who worked on the island in the early 1900s. The three principal gables of the house's southern elevation align with the three major angles of the bluff, setting off a dialogue that results in the gently bending geometry of the footprint. A pier supported by granite blocks allows access to the family's boathouse and sailboats; a guesthouse and garage, north of the main house, follows the same architectural tradition. In Maine, where houses are experienced by water as much as by land, this compound sits prominently on a well-traveled channel and, as it is exposed to the Maine elements, will weather to become an intrinsic part of the coastline to the passing sailor.

While its broad proportions stretch parallel to the long horizon, the house enjoys views in three directions and its transverse axes also culminate in the prospect of water. In plan, the hinges—or the moments where the axes shift—create the feeling of three anchored boats jostling up against one another as the sea swells. An oiled and waxed oak-paneled entrance hall sits on axis with two rocks out in the channel and connects to the west to a double-height stair hall of similar design with a bull's-eye window and beamed ceiling and the living room to the east. In larger houses from the turn of the twentieth century, architects hierarchically composed the plan to create a division between the service

and servants' areas from the main house. Today family life revolves around the kitchen and the service spaces are shared. To create a more nuanced distinction, PPA separated the guest rooms from the family's main living space. Placing the guest suite in the western portion of the house enabled independent entrances and circulation for the host and for the guest, containing the clients' experience of the house to the rooms they frequent and maintaining their privacy.

Following in the nautical vein, the library and dining room, each with multiple exposures, evoke the sensation of standing in a cockpit at sea. In Maine, where woodworking is a way of life, the interiors are a triumph in carpentry. While indigenous materials dominate—much of the wood flooring was milled from fallen oak and cherry trees from Germantown, New York—foreign materials, including the Moroccan mosaic *zillig* tile in the living room's fireplace surround, bar, and kitchen, suggest exotic travel. In the tradition of the Maine summerhouse, the south-facing porches serve as important living spaces as well as quiet, contemplative spots to revel in the scenery. The formal rooms are detailed with moldings, round arch openings, and painted paneling while others rooms display the

BELOW

With long planks reminiscent of the deck of a ship and a bull's-eye window that brings to mind a porthole, the porches take advantage of views onto Penobscot Bay and the Atlantic Ocean.

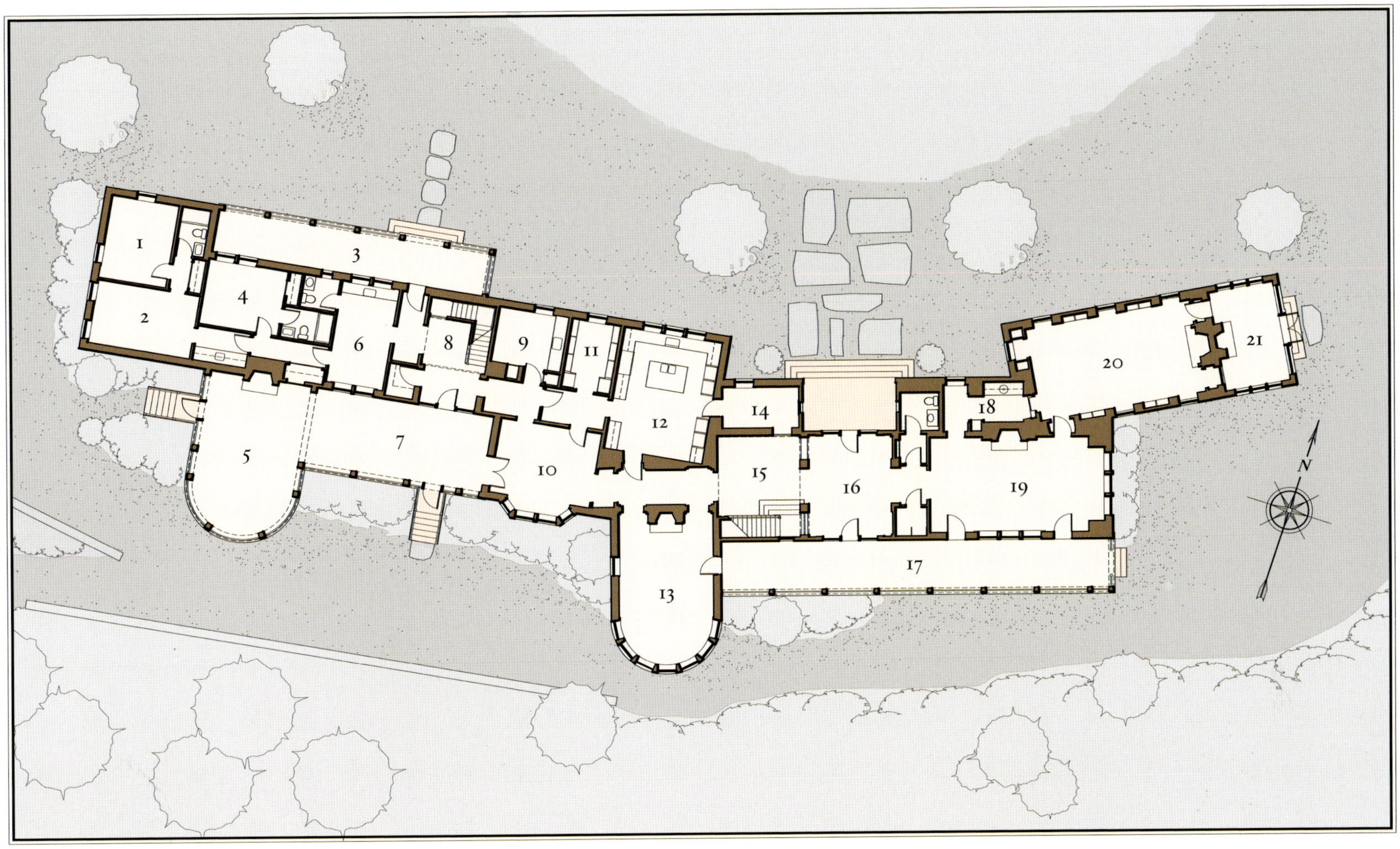

rustic simplicity of tongue-and-groove construction so redolent of the summerhouse. In the back stair hall, the ribbing of the elliptical vault easily evokes the shape of a boat's hull. Within the volumes of the house, many of the ceilings were framed to enhance the proportions of the rooms. By capturing space in the attic, for example, the master bedroom, whose design—at the client's suggestion—was influenced by the polychromed paneling of McKim, Mead & White's library in the William Watts Sherman House in Newport, Rhode Island, is anchored by a soaring tray ceiling. While many of the rooms were inspired by houses of McKim, Mead & White, their architecture has been distilled and simplified through the lens of the twenty-first century to achieve an effect similar to the work of Maine architect John Calvin Stevens, originator of the Shingle Style. Thomas Jayne's sympathetic interior decoration paired with the absence of the all-too-expected amenities now common in beach cottages—recessed lighting, air-conditioning, and AV systems—only intensify the relationship between the house and the ocean.

PLAN

The geometry of the plan responds to the angles of the bluffs and creates the feeling of three anchored ships jostling against one another.

1. Staff bedroom
2. Staff sitting room
3. Back porch
4. Bedroom
5. Screened porch
6. Mudroom
7. Screened porch
8. Back stair
9. Laundry
10. Breakfast room
11. Pantry
12. Kitchen
13. Dining room
14. Cloak room
15. Stair hall
16. Entry hall
17. Porch
18. Bar
19. Living room
20. Library
21. Office/porch

HOUSE ON PENOBSCOT BAY

BELOW

More prominent by water than by land, the design of the house follows the Shingle Style tradition of the island.

OPPOSITE BOTTOM RIGHT

A south-facing porch provides comfortable living space overlooking the ocean.

SECTION

The house is dramatically perched on the edge of the bluff, which was originally farmland.

HOUSE ON PENOBSCOT BAY ❖ 141

FAR LEFT

In the living room, a bracketed mantel with Moroccan mosaic *zillig* tile surrounds the fireplace.

LEFT

A library door disguised with bookshelves opens to reveal the bar.

OPPOSITE BOTTOM

The curved wall of windows in the dining room presents a 180-degree view of Penobscot Bay, evoking the sensation of standing on a ship at sea.

BELOW

The panoramic views of the water spill into the expansive windows in the living room.

BELOW AND RIGHT

The soaring beadboard ceiling and painted-wood paneling of the library create a pleasing contrast.

HOUSE ON PENOBSCOT BAY

SECTION

The entry hall, set on axis with two rocks out in the channel, opens into a double-height stair hall to the west.

BELOW LEFT

Small-scale paneling typical of Shingle Style inspired the design of the stair hall.

BELOW

An upstairs alcove with pocket doors opens into a quiet private bedroom with beadboard walls and a tray ceiling.

144 ❖ COUNTRY HOUSES

RIGHT

The polychrome wood-paneled master bedroom was inspired by the houses of McKim, Mead & White.

BELOW

A glimpse of the colorful paneling in the master bedroom is seen from the hall.

RIGHT

A delicate arch hovers over the bathtub, which enjoys unparalleled views.

DIAMOND A RANCH

AN UNEXPECTED OASIS OF POPLAR TREES AND ORCHARDS IN THE barren foothills of the Capitan Mountains, Diamond A Ranch is a 120,000-acre property watered by the Hondo River in central New Mexico. Over time, the additions and accumulation of various buildings and structures on the ranch had created a large and stylistically diverse compound. In its restoration and renovation, PPA chose to layer styles across the complex, weaving a narrative of historical architecture endemic to the area.

In 1964 abstract artist Herbert Bayer—Walter Gropius's favorite student at the Bauhaus—built the ranch's main house after historic drawings and designed interiors for oilman, philanthropist, and art collector Robert O. Anderson, his major client. Its facades and two-story porches loosely reproduce those of the Baca House in Upper Las Vegas, one of the masterpieces of Southwest Territorial Style—an architectural approach that developed during the West's pre-statehood days and combines aspects of Pueblo and eastern building traditions. Also, forming a portion of the living quarters were two older structures, a humble Territorial-style cottage north of the front lawn (now the servants' quarters) and the so-called Adobe Wing stretching toward the east—a historic building that once served as a way station on the stagecoach route from Lincoln to Roswell. In due time, the complex grew to embrace three more buildings: a freestanding chapel, where Bayer's abstract modernism is softened by a baroque portal and campanile salvaged from the ruins of a seventeenth-century Mexican church; a skylit windowless indoor pool pavilion with wan Victorian details; and a large freestanding structure housing storage facilities and an impressive Jacobean library paneled in Irish oak. While some of its paneling was salvaged from the turn-of-the-century Huntington Mansion in Hillsborough, California, other pieces, including the mantel's fanciful carved figures of American Indians, dated back to the late sixteenth century.

Because the compound had grown up haphazardly, the landscape was ill defined and the disjointed plan made it difficult to navigate from one wing of the house to another and to entertain on a large scale. Aside from the library, the interiors had little character or detail. The Adobe Wing had degenerated into a rabbit warren of tiny bedrooms and the main house included a vast A-framed attic, intended for the display of modern art, and

ABOVE

A balcony incorporated into a gable opens off of a guest room under the eaves.

OPPOSITE

A new door between the garden and the stone patio is pecan wood hand carved in Territorial Style.

ABOVE

The Adobe Wing, once a way station on the stagecoach route between Roswell and Lincoln, stretches east from the main house.

boxy and stark parlors and bedrooms below. To knit the Adobe Wing, pool pavilion, main house, and library together, PPA introduced a new stone-flagged patio lined on three sides by a traditional New Mexican portale, establishing a central area for outdoor entertaining. To its north, a new wing of the house contains a forty-foot living room and, on the second floor, the master bedroom suite. A new bar west of the patio lined in studded leather panels and sealed in oak echoes—without copying—the form and scale of the newly restored Jacobean Library beyond. The firm also rebuilt the pool pavilion to the east in the Greek Revival style, evoking the image of an old ballroom from the 1840s converted to a pool house in the 1920s.

With a solid knowledge of the area's history, PPA embarked on the ambitious interior program, fluidly evoking the successive stages of Lincoln County's architectural history. It carefully rebuilt the eastern guest suite in the Adobe Wing in age-old traditional materials: waxed clay and dirt floors, adobe walls richly textured with hay, and a ceiling of *vigas* and *latillas* (logs and saplings). Meanwhile, the pool pavilion, new living room, and portale columns were designed to represent a brief efflorescence of the Greek Revival in the 1840s when New Mexico became a U.S. territory and the army engineers arrived from the east with their pattern books. The main house, however, with its tinted plaster walls, harkens to the Territorial Style of the 1860s when the Greek Revival had metamorphosed into a more rustic and provincial vernacular. The master dressing suite and the third-floor guest rooms, all of which are tucked into the gabled roof, evoke an 1880s remodeling in the Railroad style—the local variant of Queen Anne architecture—while the library, the new bar, and the dining room suggest the baronial eclecticism of the early twentieth century. Thomas Jayne's decoration throughout adds another layer of texture and historical vernacular. For example, the decor of the new living room represents one era superimposed on another: a new Greek Revival parlor redecorated in the 1920s Pueblo Revival style.

Narrow channels fed by the Hondo River recall the traditional irrigation methods used by farmers in the valley to water their apple orchards; these frame the front lawn, the sunken parking area, and the terrace facing the mountains. The landscape architecture firm of Quennell Rothschild used these channels to separate the domestic landscape of the lawn and house gardens from the ranch's vast expanse of fields, pastures, and orchards.

ABOVE

The new patio, an island of indigenous stone bordered by rushing channels of water, joins the new wings of the ranch.

OVERLEAF

The glass-roofed pool pavilion in the Greek Revival style evokes the image of a ballroom transformed into a pool house in the 1920s.

LEFT

A guest room in the Adobe Wing incorporates traditional building materials including waxed clay and dirt for the floors, adobe textured with hay for the walls, and logs and saplings for the ceiling.

RIGHT

The interior of the restored modernist freestanding chapel designed by Herbert Bayer on the property is stark and white.

BELOW

The abstract modernist exterior of the chapel is embellished with a campanile salvaged from a seventeenth-century Mexican church.

PLAN

The pinwheel plan ties together various existing and new buildings and additions.

1. Kitchen
2. Pantry
3. Dining room
4. North parlor
5. Entry hall
6. South parlor
7. Spanish room
8. Bedroom
9. Bedroom
10. Bedroom
11. Pool
12. Patio
13. Bar
14. Library

OPPOSITE TOP RIGHT

Guest bedrooms tucked into the gabled roof evoke a 1880s Territorial Style and the local variant of the Queen Anne style.

OPPOSITE BOTTOM

The decorative quality of a large guest room in the Adobe Wing is created by the textures and hues of the traditional materials and white-painted trim.

TOP LEFT

The Jacobean library, the only original interior of the ranch with architectural character, was carefully restored. Its paneling was salvaged from the Huntington Mansion in Hillsborough, California, and its mantel dates to the late sixteenth century.

LEFT

A new bar paneled in studded leather evokes the scale and character of the adjoining library.

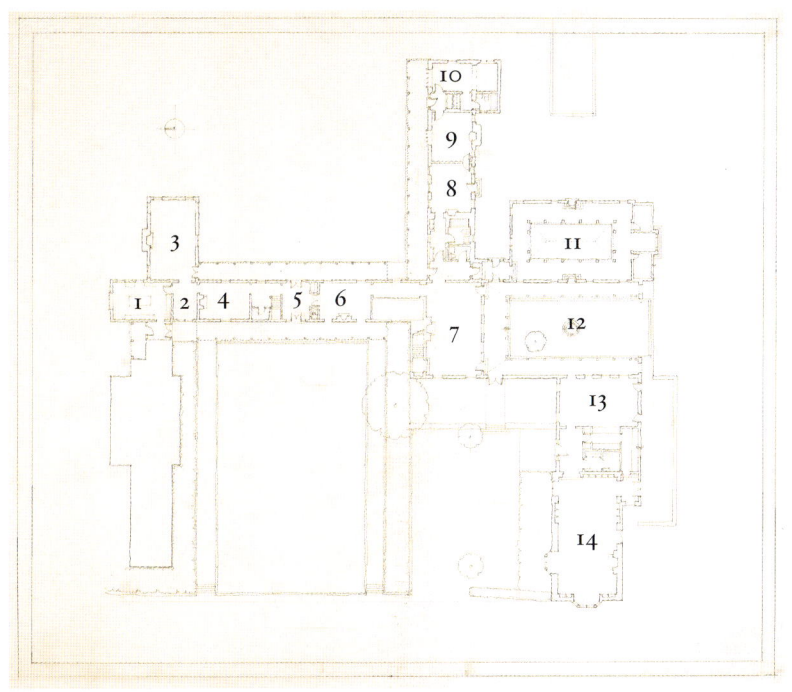

DIAMOND A RANCH ✦ 155

HOUSE IN THE SANTA LUCIA RANGE

OPPOSITE

The semielliptical dining bay opens out to stone terraces and spectacular views of the mountains.

BELOW

Decorative rafter tails embellish the roof's substantial overhang.

DRAMATIC UNENCUMBERED VIEWS OF THE SANTA LUCIA Mountains—a coastal range running between Monterey and San Luis Obispo—were central to the design of this house set within a 20,000-acre preserve. Until the 1990s, Carmel Mission cattle grazed this broad swatch of untouched land that was an operating ranch known as the Ranchos San Carlos. Its varied landscape of woodlands, savannas, and grasslands—90 percent of which is now under permanent protection—created an inspirational canvas to develop a site-specific design that sympathetically embraced both its context and the stylistic language of California's recent architectural heritage. Design guidelines and criteria imposed by the preserve's land company were detailed in their requirements for indigenous materials, traditional forms, and roof heights; it was imperative that the house recede into the landscape. PPA focused on establishing an equilibrium between the interior and exterior of the house or, in other words, maximized the experience of the site and views from within the house while minimizing the exposure and impact of the house from without.

The guidelines served as a springboard for the firm's interpretive and creative solution. Designed in the spirit of Greene & Greene and Bernard Maybeck, the one-and-a half-story 5,000-square-foot house stretches unobtrusively across a ridge with sweeping views of the mountains to the east, west, and south. It was important to preserve the essentially nineteenth-century landscape, particularly the sightlines from the neighboring homes—often miles away—and the valley below. Setting the low-lying house back from the edge of the ridge on a level clearing enabled it to blend inconspicuously with the tree line. The garage and parking area are hidden to the northeast from the living areas, deftly blocking any solar reflections that might infringe upon the outlook from the valley or from other homes.

The firm drew from California's rich architectural heritage and its store of distinctive twentieth-century houses. While the Arts and Crafts tradition inspired the low sweep of the roof and the softening effect of turned-up eaves, Asian styles endemic to the region informed the exposed cedar fascia and skirt boards, which create a seasoned texture in contrast to the slate shingle of the hipped roofs and cedar shingles of the walls. Decorative rafter tails form the substantial overhang that shades the house in the sunny and

dry summer months. As intended, with exposure to the elements over time, the palette of natural materials of the lower walls and posts will weather faster than the cedar under the eaves, creating an organic effect, as if the house grew up as a natural extension of its site.

An entrance courtyard planted with colorful specimens captures the light and charm of the wooded grassy areas to the north; the stone fountain is set on axis with the front entrance, framed by natural cedar porch posts and embellished by a clerestory level. While the entrance court is intimate and enclosed, the balance of the house opens dramatically to the views. The thin U-shaped plan allows the unfettered light of the expansive California skies to filter inside, creating bright and elegant spaces. The interiors, decorated by Paul Wiseman, unfold in a succession of fluid simplicity created by the contrast of painted walls and teak details. This approach, carried throughout, creates a neutral background that, rather than competing with the views, invites it inside. The entrance hall, lit by clerestory windows, opens into a large informal teak-ceilinged living room, which is subtly differentiated from the windowed dining bay by a varied ceiling height, distilled forms of teak columns, and bowed details. The kitchen, garages, and one-and-a-half-story guest suite occupy the eastern section of the house while a master suite, study, and adjoining bedroom round out the plan to the west. With French doors and large paned windows, all of the rooms—from the dining bay to the wood-paneled master bathroom—have an immediate relationship with the outdoors. One only has to open a door, from any room, to be outside, where cedar and stone terraces, a pool, and gardens designed by Suzman Design Associates bask in the spectacular scenery of the surrounding mountains and valleys.

ABOVE

The cedar terrace off of the master bedroom and bath wends around the bluff.

OPPOSITE

The subtle color variations of the slate add texture to the shifting rooflines of the garage and guest wing.

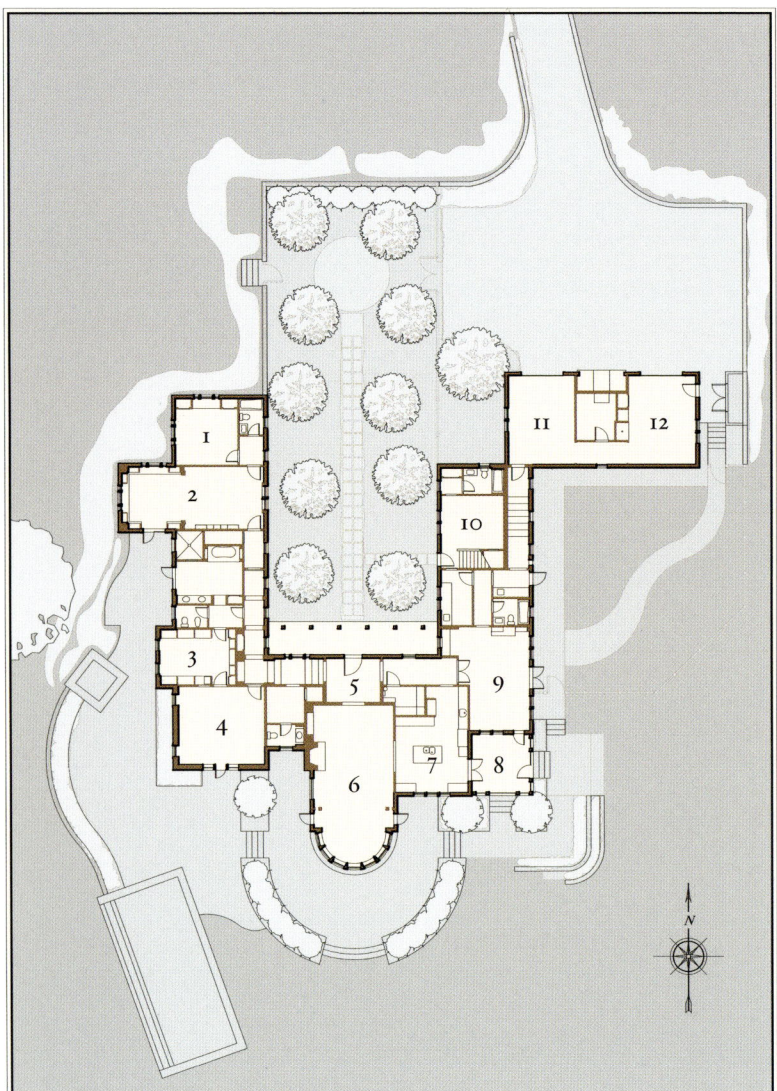

ABOVE

A stone walkway leads through the front garden to the main entrance, which is framed by natural cedar porch posts.

PLAN

The U-shaped plan allows light to enter the house from all directions and creates an enclosed garden approach from the north.

1. Bedroom
2. Study
3. Dressing room
4. Master bedroom
5. Entry hall
6. Living room
7. Kitchen
8. Screened porch
9. Sitting room
10. Guest suite
11. Garage
12. Garage

RIGHT

The natural palette of materials enables the house to blend unobtrusively into the landscape.

OPPOSITE

Custom teak cabinetry and a copper hood add to the warmth of the kitchen.

OPPOSITE BOTTOM

The living room, with a tent-form ceiling, is centered on a mantel with a tiled and hammered-copper surround.

RIGHT

The oval opening to the teak coffered ceiling centers the architecture of the front hall.

BELOW RIGHT

The double-height front hall opens directly into the living room and the views beyond.

BELOW

The teak door and window frames create a rhythm against the light-colored walls.

MEADOW LANE HOUSE

ABOVE
Steps lead from the entrance vestibule up to the main hall and views of the ocean.

OPPOSITE
Perched on the dunes, the asymmetrical shingled mass responds to the landscape and encompasses both old and new volumes.

SET ON A NARROW STRIP OF LAND BETWEEN SHINNECOCK BAY and the Atlantic Ocean, this oceanfront house previously consisted of a collection of nondescript stucco bungalows and additions essentially perched on top of the dunes. In arriving at a design solution, PPA was presented with the difficult challenge of tying together the various often-unrelated masses of an unremarkable existing structure under a close schedule and strict design regulations. The house's extraordinary location was unrivaled; however, to tear it down and build anew would have required a setback from the shore that would have robbed it of its most defining characteristic. As mandated by the town, there could be no change to the footprint on the ocean side. This regulatory measure dictated the shape and trajectory of the building and prompted expansion northward and upward, bringing the house to 12,000 square feet and two stories.

Designed and built within a year, the otherwise unexceptional house was transformed into something compositionally fluid, livable, and appropriate to its seaside setting by new massing that encompassed new and old volumes, cedar shingles overlaid with restrained classical details, and open porches. With the exception of pediments marking entries, PPA suppressed the use of classical vocabulary, letting the play between the shingled volumes and white-painted trim emerge as the decorative quality. The jogs that were maintained in the roofline reflect the accretive quality of the former house and the movement of the plan in section. The client was partial to some of the quirky qualities of the existing house—a result of its haphazard growth over time—and wanted to retain them. Also on the client's wish list was a tower room, a contemplative space where the site's remarkable vistas could be experienced in their entirety.

To accentuate the beautiful setting, PPA developed a site-specific design in which the relationship between the house and its surroundings were emphasized. From the westernmost sunroom, French doors open onto the porch and a double set of steps, which lead down to a brick pool terrace and cedar pergola hewn of heavy logs. The axis of the front entrance culminates with access to the beach. Well screened from its neighbors to the east and west, the property is imbued with a sense of privacy, enhanced by Deborah Nevins's gardens and parterres. Nevins's scheme divides the northwestern section of the

grounds—the only portion of the site with closed views—into a set of outdoor rooms with edges developed as colorful borders in the spirit of Beatrix Farrand.

Shifts in levels, one of the aspects the client had liked, were a carryover from the pre-existing house that added charm and personality to the plan. From the entrance hall, a run of steps ascends to the main hall with a formal living room to the west and sunroom beyond and the main stair to the second floor to the east. From this upper hall, a short set of steps descends east to an octagonal dining room and yet another set leads to the kitchen, breakfast room, guest rooms, and library paneled in faux-bois knotty pine. In Beaux-Arts fashion, strong axes were established to organize and pull together the rooms. One axis ties the main stair to the formal living room while cross axes run between the stair and octagonal dining room and from the front entrance through the main hall to the porch and dunes. As it had at the House on Penobscot Bay, the firm established the entrance to the first-floor guest suite independently from the main circulation of the house, providing privacy for both host and guest and containing the client's experience of the rooms to the spaces they use. Bright neutral colors and decoration by Thomas Jayne create a fitting backdrop for the clean lines and classical detailing. Inside, like the outside, architectural rhetoric was subdued in shaping fresh and bright enveloping spaces that bring in the sun and sea. On the new second floor, a gallery of windows lights the stair hall, which leads into the large master suite. And, from the second floor, a hidden staircase rises up into the tower room where walls of windows capture the view in four directions: along Meadow Lane, over the dunes, out to a meandering inlet off of Shinnecock Bay, and to the marshy unsettled land of the DuPont Sanctuary.

ABOVE

The carved-wood living room mantel is distilled from classical examples.

ABOVE LEFT

The tower room enjoys 360-degree views of the ocean, bay, and surrounding landscape.

OPPOSITE

A gallery of windows on the second floor lights the landing at the center of the open enfilade that runs through the house.

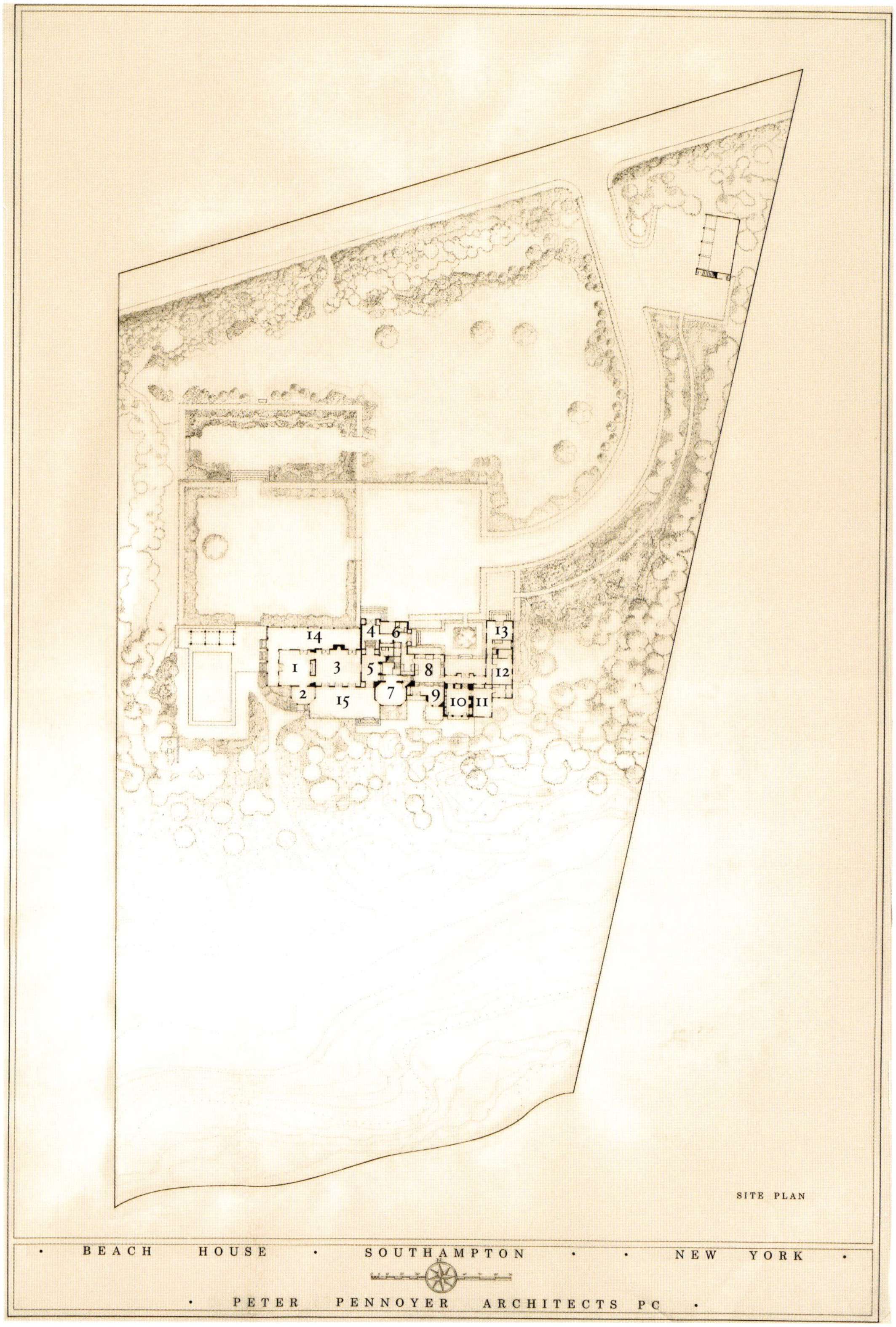

SITE PLAN

· BEACH HOUSE · SOUTHAMPTON · NEW YORK ·
· PETER PENNOYER ARCHITECTS PC ·

PLAN

The rooms are organized around axes that relate to the gardens, pool, and paths to the beach.

1. Sun room
2. Turkish corner
3. Living room
4. Entry hall
5. Hall
6. Stair hall
7. Foyer
8. Study
9. Breakfast room
10. Library
11. Bedoom
12. Bedoom
13. Bedoom
14. Porch
15. Porch

OPPOSITE TOP
The northwest portion of the property is divided into a series of outdoor rooms lined with colorful flowerbeds.

RIGHT
The decorative quality of the facades emerges from the play of shingle and white-painted trim.

OAKLEY FARM

A RARE EXAMPLE OF A HIGH ITALIANATE HOUSE IN VIRGINIA, Oakley Farm was a special project that provided the opportunity for PPA to examine the relationship between restoring important historic architecture and designing new additions that updated the house and harmonized with the existing structure. Located in the rolling hills of Virginia's hunt country, west of Washington D.C., it is set on a gradual rise in the scenic and storied landscape of fox hunting, steeplechases, and generations-old farms. The property's 1857 Italianate villa, based on the popular pattern book *The Modern Architect* by Philadelphia-based architect Samuel Sloan, was built by Richard Henry Dulany of Welbourne in the nearby town of Middleburg, founder of the all-important Upperville Colt and Horse Show. During the Civil War, the farm's 450 acres set the stage for skirmishes between Union troops and Mosby's Rangers, a battalion of partisan cavalry that covertly operated in the area under General Robert E. Lee. Very much a local landmark, Oakley was later owned by Dr. Archibald Cary Randolph and his wife Theodora Ayer Randolph, the current owner's grandmother. Mrs. Randolph, an accomplished horsewoman, succeeded her husband as master of the Piedmont Hunt, the 150-year-old landowner's association, and was known among her peers as the first lady of foxhunting.

By the time Oakley fell into its current hands, the family estate had descended into a retired state and its interiors, once gloriously decorated by Sister Parish, were in need of an overhaul. As originally designed after Sloan's model, the house was incomplete; the absence of moldings and decorative architectural details—elements that can infuse a room with a certain texture and depth—left the interiors unfinished. Additionally, a number of haphazard additions had upset the T-shaped house's symmetrical balance and post–Civil War infill, particularly in the rear porch, had rendered the double-height veranda an awkward jumble of columns and appendages.

With a clear history of the building and its context, PPA developed a design that sufficiently modernized the house to accommodate a family with three small children but also preserved its iconic Italianate character and its nineteenth-century quirks. The existing pink stucco exterior was restored to the original sand-colored shade with

OPPOSITE

New details such as the arcaded lantern completed the High Italianate restoration and renovation of this originally unfinished 1857 villa.

BELOW

The third-floor lantern lights the curving form of the original stair, dramatically welcoming visitors into the entryway and stair hall, which connects the east and west parlors.

gray aggregate. In some cases the design entailed improving upon what had been there or re-establishing what had been compromised through the progression of time. To recapture the original poetic templelike expression of the rear elevation, the pediment on the two-story veranda was widened to embrace five bays, rather than three; one of the chimneys was moved to reinforce the centered elevation. Much in the spirit of Nottoway (1859) in White Castle, Louisiana, the colossal Italianate order—a Dulany family motif modeled on the columns and entablature of Mount Vernon—was reestablished by recessing the balustrades and cornices of the porch behind the planes of the post. With the exception of relocating the kitchen from the basement to the first floor, the plan of the house essentially remained true to its traditional center hall configuration. To differentiate the newly designed spaces from the historic portion of the house, PPA used large windows in the kitchen and Tudor Gothic arches—inspired by Calvert Vaux's conservatory designs—in the basement mudroom refit with encaustic tile. This subtle distinction underlines and honors the growth of a house over time. A new red painted tern roof—also a feature of the estate's various outbuildings—reflects the local vernacular.

Inside, new moldings, cornices, and decorative ceilings give the rooms, decorated by Katie Ridder, a compositional order and scale. A stair leading to the third floor, where a laundry room and cistern had once been located, was secreted away and a new arcaded lantern embellished with oak leaves and anthemia, designed more in the spirit of Sir John Soane than Samuel Sloan, turned the central stair hall into a pivotal moment, filling the previously dark center of the house with ample daylight.

From the rear porch, a new stair leads down to a path connecting the house to a series of lawn terraces and gardens designed by Madison Cox and beyond to the pastures and the property's extensive acreage. The grounds include a guest cottage, a renovated 1830s summer kitchen with vertical board and white painted batten siding, raised-seam tern roof, and details designed in the vein of A. J. Downing. The firm adopted the vocabulary of an 1830s farm building for the design of the new adjacent pool house, a building that also doubles as a ballroom. Its Colonial Revival interior evokes the patina of a farm building renovated the 1920s. Its pocket doors slide back, opening the lofty space to porches—designed in the Federal style—and the greenery of Virginia's hunt country.

ABOVE

The property also includes a summer kitchen from the 1830s, renovated into a guest cottage, and a series of lawn terraces and gardens designed by Madison Cox.

OPPOSITE TOP

An entrance portico leads into the pool house, designed in the spirit a renovated 1830s farm building.

OPPOSITE BOTTOM

The Colonial Revival interior of the pool house evokes the grandeur of a 1920s ballroom.

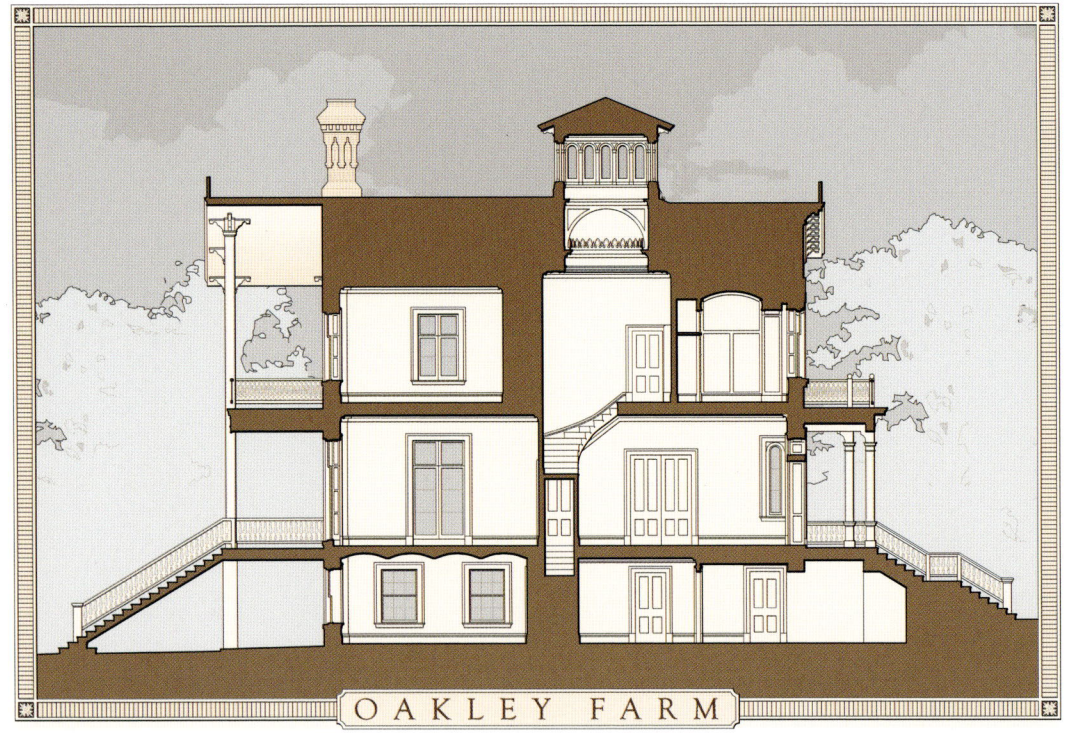

OAKLEY FARM

174 ❖ COUNTRY HOUSES

SECTION

The new arcaded lantern, which incorporates space on the third floor once occupied by a laundry room and cistern, creates a natural light source for the previously dark stair hall.

OPPOSITE TOP RIGHT

On the east facade, the large windows of the kitchen and Tudor Gothic arches of the basement mudroom differentiate newly designed spaces from the historic fabric of the house.

OPPOSITE BOTTOM

To recapture the templelike expression of the rear elevation, the pediment of the two-story rear veranda was widened to embrace five bays.

BELOW

Designed in the spirit of Sir John Soane, the soaring lantern is detailed with oak leaves and anthemia.

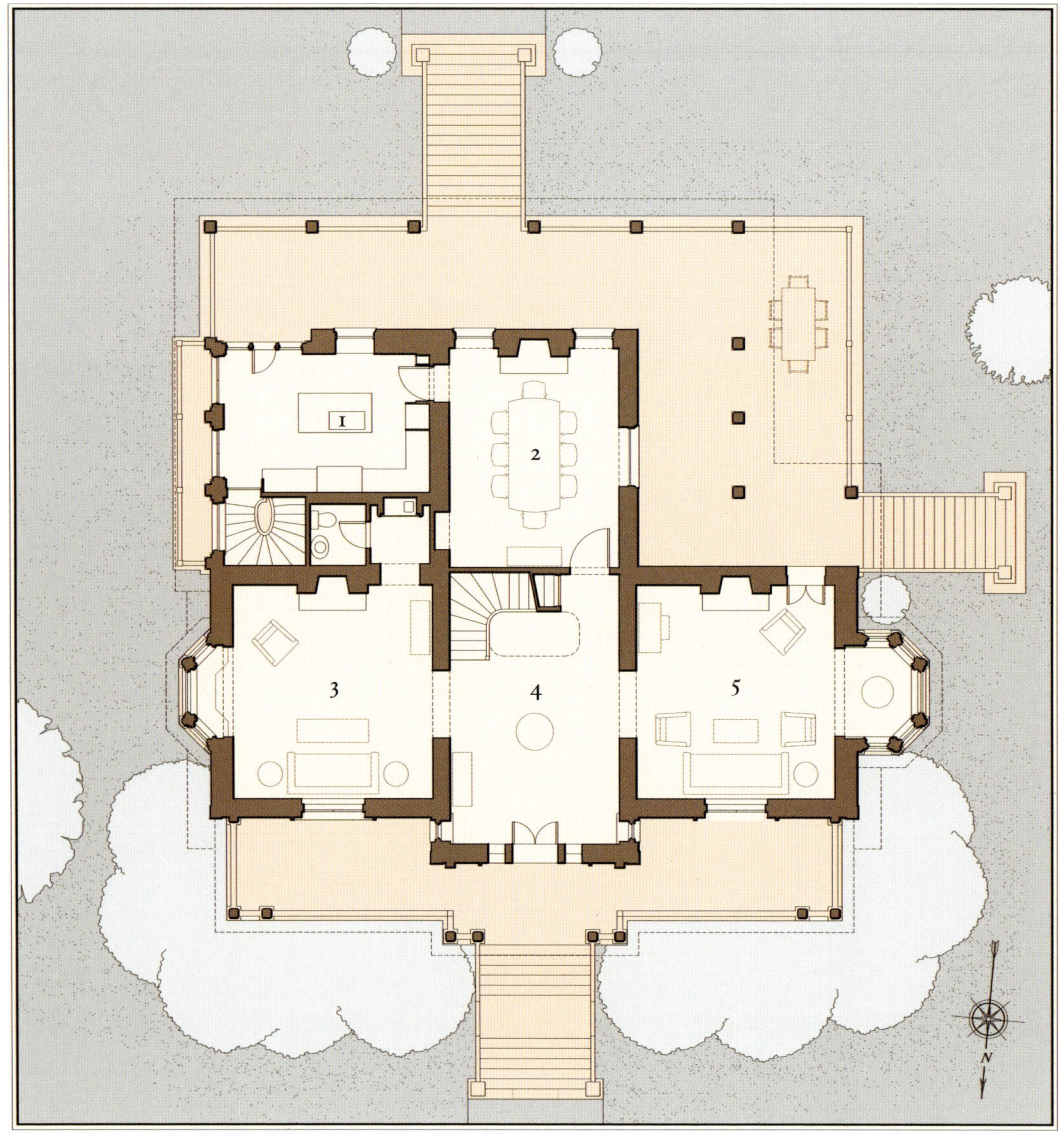

ABOVE

The encaustic-tiled mudroom connects to the kitchen above with a new stair in the spirit of the main stair.

ABOVE LEFT

The soaring space of the kitchen enjoys access to the terrace through tall French doors.

PLAN

The first-floor plan, consisting of a stair hall, east and west parlors, dining room, and kitchen, shows the many connections to verandas and the stairs to the gardens.

1. Kitchen
2. Dining room
3. East parlor
4. Entry hall
5. West parlor

OPPOSITE

In the west parlor, a decorative ceiling and moldings complete the interior architecture of the room.

OVERLEAF

The raised-seam red painted tern roof of the pool house and main house behind reflects the local vernacular. The pool house also mimics the five-bay porch of the original house.

FEDERAL HOUSE

OPPOSITE
Revealing the intricacies of geometry, the entrance facade, located to the east on the long side of the house, displays a two-to-one ratio of clapboard siding.

BELOW
Delicately carved fluted columns support the recessed entrance portico.

LOCATED IN AN IMPORTANT HISTORIC AREA FIRST DEVELOPED during the pre-Revolutionary period, this new house reflects the rich architectural heritage of its surroundings. Elegant Georgian houses with refined decorative details conveying of their inhabitants' elevated social standing distinguish the streets of this neighborhood, and some have even borne witness to important events in America's early history. Many of the later houses, built during the nineteenth and early twentieth centuries—some of which were designed by well-known architects—reflect the ongoing narrative of changing American tastes and styles through time.

This project presented PPA the opportunity to design a house in a prestigious area that has seen little new construction since the postwar era. The previous building on the site—a charming but unremarkable 1810 clapboard house renovated in the 1890s—had burned to the ground. While the local historical commission strictly regulates alterations to existing buildings, there were no limits placed on this newly cleared site. In its design, PPA chose to embrace and improve upon the historic context and the established architectural character of the distinguished surrounding houses. The new scheme, roughly the same size as the previous house, evoked stylistic qualities of the Federal style, refined and reworked to meet the needs of a twenty-first-century family. Like many of the nearby Georgian and Federal examples, the design presents a symmetrical facade to the street, its long axis extending back through the site. The primary elevation of the preexisting house, while essentially following the same footprint, had been oriented to the east, rather than the south, and had not been open to the Fletcher Steele–designed garden set slightly above the street. Steele, perhaps best known for his gardens at Naumkeag in Stockbridge, Massachusetts, designed a small oasis enclosed by a curved retaining wall in 1947 for the current owner, which provided a sense of privacy within the streetscape. In the new design, PPA maintained the integrity of Steele's garden and centered the house and its elliptical porch, embellished with the Tower of the Winds order, on its curved wall. In the spirit of the New England vernacular, the wood facades revel in the subtle variations of texture and linearity. Here PPA sought to create the effect of an etching, which also reveals itself through the subtle play of light, shadow, and line.

ABOVE

Column capitals are designed after the order found at the Tower of the Winds, a marble clock tower on the Roman agora in Athens.

The intricacies of its geometry are expressed in the two-to-one ratio of the clapboard siding and quoins (the decorative trim along the corners of the house carved to resemble stone).

Inside, the plan breaks from the typical center hall layout of Georgian and Federal–style houses; while the south portico on the street creates the impression of a front door, the main entrance lies along the east elevation. Here an axis extends through a mirrored foyer with poured-glass casings and silver-leaf panel moldings underneath the sweep of the curved stair—a reincarnation of Steele's elliptical garden—though the stair hall and into the dining room. Steele's garden anchors the major north–south axis through the porch, living room, and stair hall, which then extends back to the mudroom, back stair, kitchen and family room—the informal family-friendly living space desired by the client. The previous house on the site had a detached garage that took up much of the rear of the property; PPA buried the garage underground, freeing up yard space and creating a platform to the north for terraces off the family room. A laylight wrought with an ironwork pattern inspired by Delano & Aldrich lights the stair hall, which lies at the heart of the plan. On the second floor, a bull's-eye window set into the curve of the wall looks onto a study and filters additional light from the outside. Throughout, a lightness of touch and attenuated proportions, as inspired by Federal antecedents, permeates the details—the moldings and door-and-window casings—giving the interiors an elegant expression.

OPPOSITE TOP LEFT
An analytique drawing of the south facade details the design of the architrave, widow's walk railing, and column capital.

OPPOSITE TOP RIGHT
Following the example of nearby Georgian and Federal-style houses, this house presents a symmetrical facade to the street but its French doors, central portico, and pediment sets it apart from its neighbors.

ABOVE
In the spirit of the New England vernacular, the main facade revels in the subtle variations of texture and linearity and the play of light and shadow that bring to mind an early-nineteenth-century etching.

OPPOSITE

The overdoors and decorative plaster ceiling in the dining room were inspired by Federal precedent.

RIGHT

The primary axis through the house runs from the curved Fletcher Steele-designed garden through the living room and stair hall, back though the mudroom to the family room.

1. Living room
2. Dining room
3. Kitchen
4. Family room
5. Library
6. Study
7. Stair hall
8. Foyer
9. Mudroom

BELOW

The kitchen is a contemporary departure from the more traditional interiors.

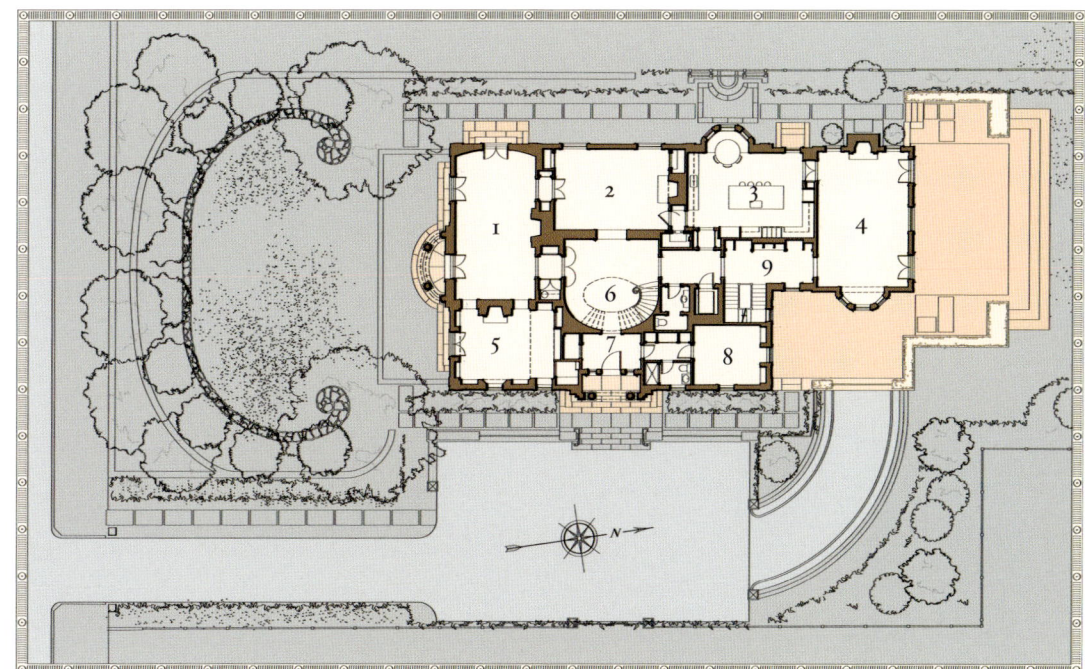

LEFT
David Adler's powder room at the Reed estate in Lake Forest, Illinois, provided the inspiration for the mirrored foyer with poured-glass moldings.

OPPOSITE
The floating stair curves up around the foyer entrance and is embellished by a display niche, a handrail with bronze accents, and a bull's-eye window drawing light from an upstairs study.

OPPOSITE

Two doors with hand-carved Adamesque details in the elegant plaster-paneled living room open into the oak-paneled library beyond.

RIGHT

The stair hall is lit by a laylight detailed with an abstracted classical pattern designed in the spirit of Delano & Aldrich.

BELOW

The mudroom with built-in cubbies for children's coats and storage also serves as a back stair hall.

BEACH HOUSE

OPPOSITE

The open-air sleeping porch and widow's walk, seen through cypress and juniper trees, make this the quintessential summerhouse.

BELOW

Asymmetrical window placement and a bull's-eye window add a sense of spontaneity to the front facade, balanced by two sheared gables and a central eyebrow dormer.

ONCE A LARGE WATERFRONT FARM DATING TO 1682, MISHAUM Point, a narrow and windswept slip of land that juts south into Buzzards Bay, transformed into a summer colony at the turn of the twentieth century. Boston architect William Ralph Emerson, best known for his Victorian-era cottages and seaside inns, designed a number of weathered-shingle gambrel-roofed houses that hug the perimeter of the peninsula. Having spent his summers on the point—his family had been entrenched in the community for generations—Peter Pennoyer was well aware of Mishaum's distinctive architectural tradition This Shingle-style house, located on land once occupied by a prefabricated makeshift World War II–era cottage, inspired the opportunity to translate the innate qualities of the existing nineteenth-century summerhouses—which give Mishaum its special sense of place—into an entirely new design.

Here PPA aspired to capture something of the informal and whimsical elegance of the age-old summerhouse organically realized over time, drawing inspiration from Emerson's nearby work. Clad in white cedar shingles with a red cedar Dutch gambrel roof, this 6,000-square-foot house is solid and balanced and, despite its size, without pretense—a significant goal of the project. The clients desired the house to be instilled with "spontaneity" and a sense of "spirituality." The clear symmetry of the entrance facade, marked by a pair of sheared gables, is set against the seemingly impulsive placement of a bull's-eye, which lights the stair landing. Details such as the entrance portico embellished with exaggerated latticework, a large eyebrow dormer, and a widow's walk lend depth and vitality but are understated so they do not overpower the facades and delicate play of materials and window patterns. The rear porch, designed at just the right depth and height to capture the summer light; the upstairs bedrooms; and the beaded fir-lined sleeping porch, accessed by a hidden staircase, enjoy views east of the property's beach, sheltered by cypress and juniper trees and, in the distance, the Elizabeth Islands.

The interiors, decorated by Katie Ridder, reflect the relaxed atmosphere of a traditional summerhouse with a collection of family furniture and rustic antiques amassed through generations. To encourage a sense of spontaneity and organic growth more inherent in older homes, PPA incorporated various shifts in floor level and ceiling

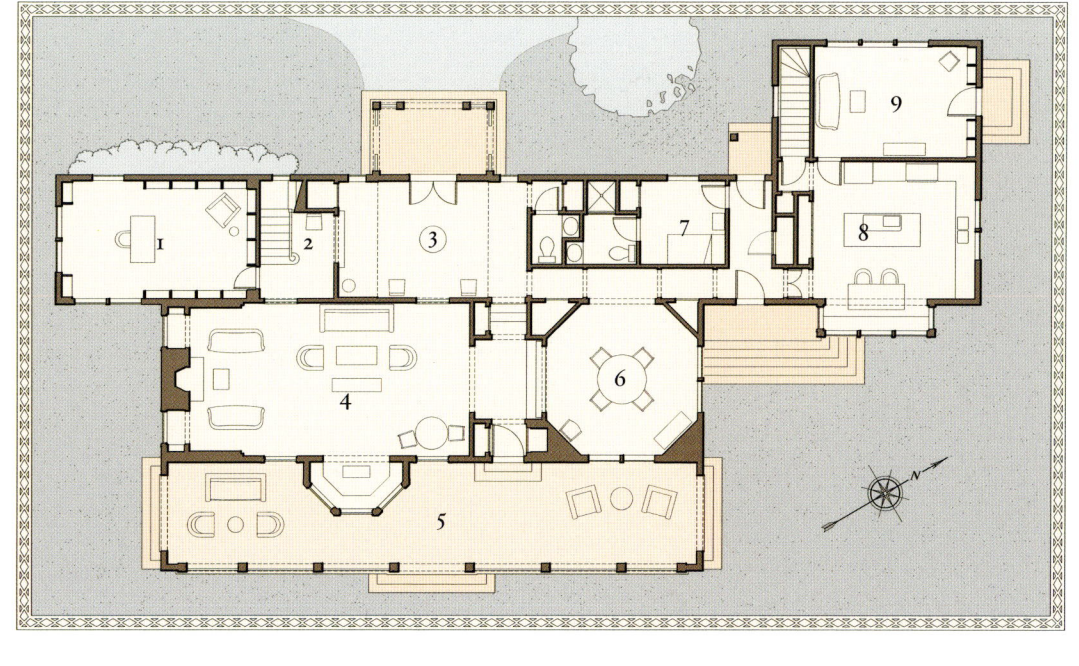

LEFT

A colonnaded porch overlooks the lawn, once used as pasture land, to sweeping views of Buzzard's Bay beyond.

PLAN

Unexpected room shapes and angles are contained within the house's rectilinear plan.

1. Study
2. Stair hall
3. Entry hall
4. Living room
5. Porch
6. Dining room
7. Staff room
8. Kitchen
9. Family room

height to give the section a charming liveliness. Shaping the interior architecture in such a way creates unexpected angles and perspective changes throughout the rooms. From the double-height paneled entrance hall—papered with a William Morris print and lit from the second-floor gallery—steps lead down into a large living room with a beadboard ceiling, generous bay window, and galleried openings onto the stair and entrance halls one level higher. The firm set the octagonal corner dining room on axis with the living room but placed it two steps up and embellished the ceiling with beadboard arranged as a series of wedges. Accessed through the living room or from a hallway leading to the kitchen and family room wing, the room reveals itself to visitors as they move through the house, its perfect geometry unfolding as if in a moment of fortuitous happenchance.

The grounds, landscaped by Horiuchi & Solien, include a guest cottage and garage. PPA designed a simple parterre defined by a dry stack wall to contain the lawn on the old pastureland that rolls down to the rocky beach.

BEACH HOUSE ✱ 193

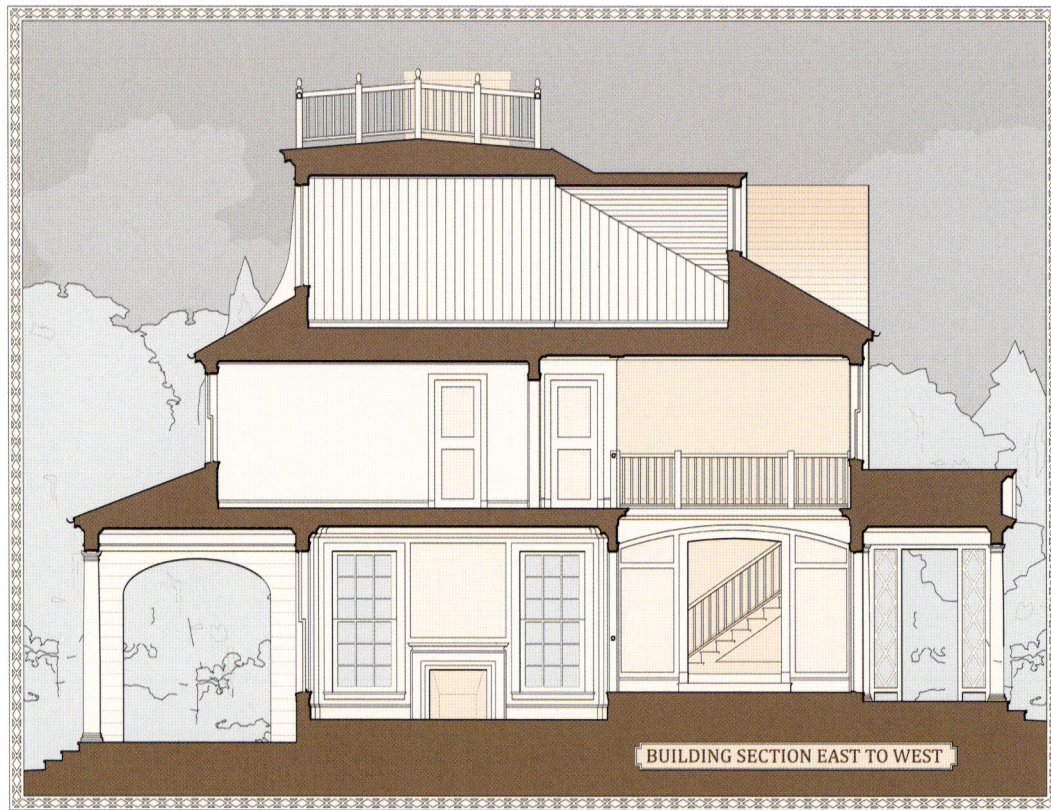

BUILDING SECTION EAST TO WEST

ABOVE
A bull's-eye window lights the double-height paneled entry hall, with a bridgelike landing connecting to the second-floor gallery.

RIGHT
The living room was designed to incorporate an elaborate rug hooked by the owner's mother.

SECTION
The varying floor levels and ceiling heights give the house an organic quality, as if it was expanded over time.

OPPOSITE
Steps lead to the octagonal dining room where a beadboard ceiling, articulated as eight wedges, echoes the unique shape of the room.

DRUMLIN HALL

OCATED IN THE VERDANT AND ROLLING LANDSCAPE OF EASTERN Dutchess County, an area of the Hudson Valley settled with open fields and horse farms, Drumlin Hall is a new classical stone house whose name is drawn from the dramatic setting in a valley of miniature hills—or drumlins—that were formed by glacial deposits. Much like rural England, this hamlet near Millbrook, New York, is steeped in a shroud of gentility where activities such as game hunting and polo are favored leisure pursuits. Conceived as a square Palladian villa, this 7,500-square-foot house, echoing the client's deep admiration of the architecture of Robert Adam and the craftsmanship of Duncan Phyfe, sits as comfortably here as it would in England's pastoral greens.

In Drumlin Hall, PPA sought to design something of a jewel box—a slightly feminine house that would reflect the historic character of its surroundings and simultaneously set off and appropriate the client's museum-quality collections of nineteenth-century American art and Federal-style furniture. The exterior, faced in warm buff sandstone carved by artisans in China, is a lesson in balance, symmetry, and harmonious proportion and bows to the wealth of Regency houses set forth by such architects as Henry Holland, Benjamin Latrobe, Sir John Soane, and S. P. Cockerell. The four principal facades—each with its own distinct personality—delight in the possibilities of geometry, graceful proportion, and equilibrium. The firm emphasized the Neoclassical spirit of the pedimented south facade commanding the long approach and distinguished it with French doors, lunettes carved with bas-relief cornucopias, urns, and massive chimney stacks. PPA centered the western entrance facade on a gently arched porte cochere inspired by Montgomery Place, designed by A. J. Davis in nearby Annandale-on-Hudson, and created a more romantic and heroically scaled facade to the north, where the shifting planes of the two severe wings, columned bay of the breakfast room, and massive center chimney create a delicate play of volumes expressive of the important central vaulted space within. A round portico anchoring the east facade opens off of the living room out to the landscape.

The plan of the house revolves around two central axes and succinctly absorbs all of the rooms into a contained rectangle with windows that express themselves symmetrically on the facades. From the porte cochere a recessed front door leads into a groin-vaulted

OPPOSITE

Drumlin Hall is dramatically set within a valley of miniature hills or drumlins.

ABOVE

Imported Silk Road sandstone carved by local artisans in China comprises the portico of the east facade.

PLAN

The plan is organized around two central axes; all of the rooms fall into place with windows that express themselves symmetrically on the facades like a well-conceived puzzle.

1. Kitchen
2. Breakfast room
3. Dining room
4. Entry hall
5. Stair hall
6. Gun room
7. Bar
8. Library
9. Drawing room

foyer through to the stair hall, where the axis continues through the drawing room to the porch with views of a river and hidden valley beyond. At the same time, PPA organized an equally powerful axis connecting the great sweeping semi-cylindrical stair to the library and its south-facing vistas over the Hudson Valley and contained the experience of moving through the rooms, from one to the next, with a secondary donut circulation. At the heart of the house lies the groin-vaulted stair hall, which doubles as a gallery, its white-painted walls primed to display the client's Hudson River School and American Impressionist paintings. On the second floor, a large vaulted space lit by a laylight at the center of a handkerchief dome centers the space and bedrooms echo the fluid movement of the public rooms below. PPA designed the circulation of the house to relate to these two large central spaces and the layout of the rooms seems to fall effortlessly into place from there.

Attention to detail throughout reinforces the classical essence of the house. In the stair hall, Greek Revival–inspired door casings, pilasters, and standing door pediments

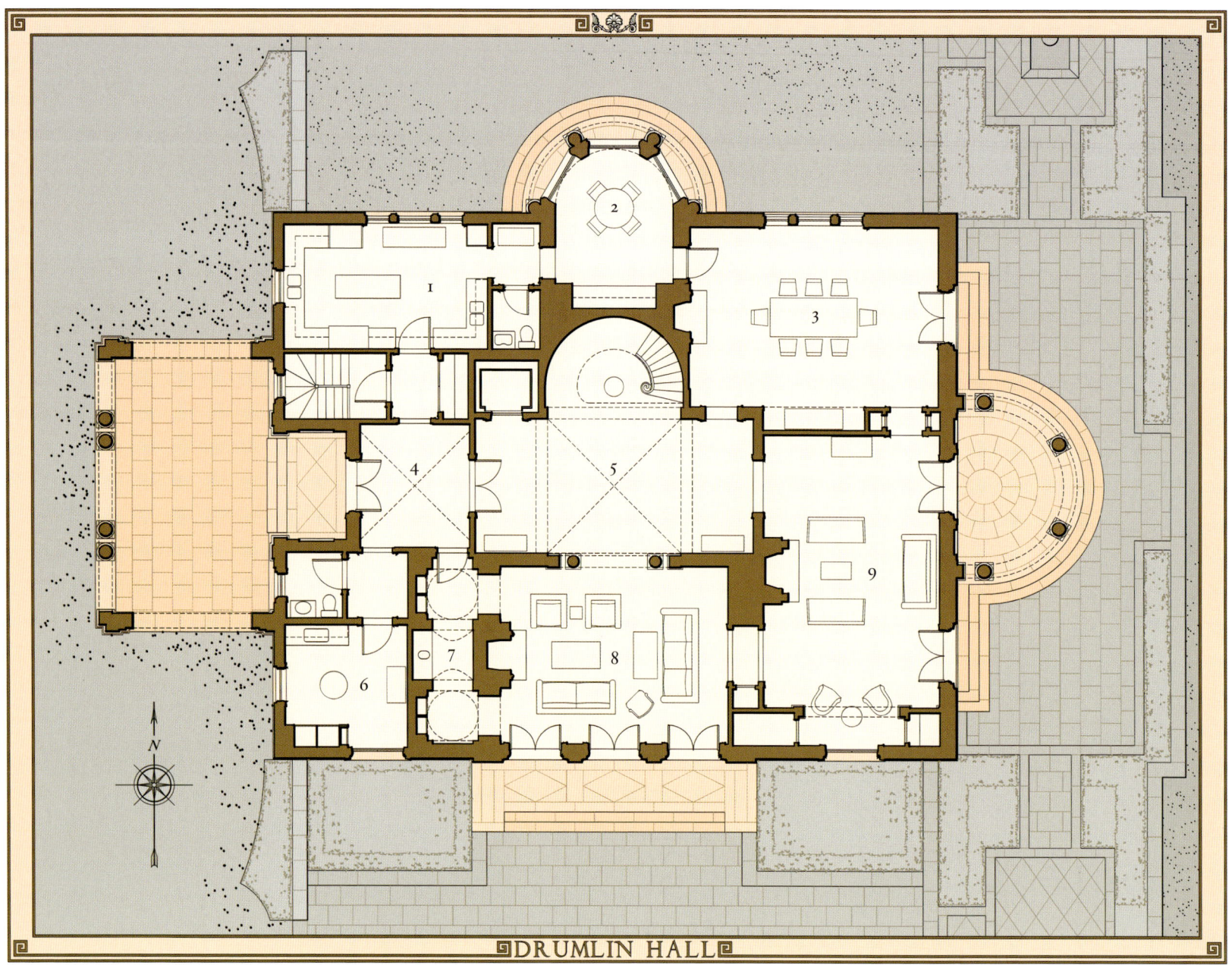

carved with anthemia mark the entryways set along the long axis while a set of faux-marble columns frame the library. PPA designed the drawing room around an Italian mantel from the 1820s elaborately carved with vestal virgins and Mercury; it evokes the work of Minard Lafever, which influenced the design for the door casings and Aeolic pilasters. Similarly, PPA scaled the dining room around a late-eighteenth-century wood mantel from Philadelphia, perhaps imported from England, finely carved with figures of Dionysus, grapes, and bucranium, its delicate fluting serving as inspiration for the fluted doorframes. The faux bois library connects, through small domed book recesses on either side of the fireplace, back to a bar concealed behind the chimneybreast, where bead moldings articulated in gold leaf express the vaults. PPA wove details such as a repeated star motif, a nod to the client's Texas heritage, to personalize the design. Painted wood floors in the stair halls, bar, and library reference other important historic houses in the area, such as Edgewater. In carrying out the great curving stair, the firm looked to Cheekwood, the Cheek estate in Nashville, Tennessee—a house the client admired. It refined the composition and scale of Cheekwood's antique balustrade adorning the sweeping central stair to fit the proportions of Drumlin Hall and brought on metalworker Jean Wiart to execute a delicately wrought pattern of garlands, pine cones, and eagles. In the upstairs stair hall, the most dramatic interior in the house, the firm incorporated niches for sculpture—as it did in the stair—fusing art with architecture. The hall accesses four bedrooms, including the master suite with hand-painted paper by De Gournay based on nineteenth-century aquatints and personalized with nearby landmarks, such as Olana and Montgomery Place. The decoration of the rooms, sensitively carried out by Thomas Jayne, reinforces the classical nature of the design, the art collection, and the antique furniture.

ABOVE

The shifting planes of the heroically scaled north facade encompass a massive center chimney.

SECTION

All of the rooms in the house, as revealed in the east-west section, relate to the vaulted galleries on the first and second floors.

OVERLEAF

The east-facing portico and terrace overlook the open fields and rolling farmland of eastern Dutchess County.

202 ❖ COUNTRY HOUSES

OPPOSITE TOP LEFT

An antique balustrade at Cheekwood, the Cheek estate in Nashville, Tennessee, served as inspiration for the embellishment of Drumlin Hall's sweeping stair.

OPPOSITE BOTTOM LEFT

Jean Wiart carried out the balustrade's intricate pattern of garlands, pinecones, and eagles.

OPPOSITE RIGHT

The painted wood floor in the first-floor gallery recalls the stair hall at Edgewater, an 1825 estate attributed to Robert Mills in Barrytown, New York.

RIGHT

With niches and expansive wall space, the top-lit second-floor hall acts as a gallery to display Hudson River School art.

BELOW

A computer-generated wire diagram reveals the complex geometries of the vaulted galleries and elliptical stair.

DRUMLIN HALL ✳ 203

FAR LEFT

Faux-marble columns frame the entrance into the library where three sets of French doors open to the south.

LEFT

Gold-leaf bead moldings articulate the vaults in the bar.

BELOW

Two domed book recesses in the faux-bois paneled library connect to the bar, concealed behind the chimneybreast.

OPPOSITE ALL

The details in the drawing room, which was scaled around a 1820s Italian mantel carved with figures of vestal virgins and Mercury, evoke the work of Minard Lafever.

TOP LEFT

Thomas Jayne decorated the walls of the bedroom with hand-painted De Gournay paper, based on nineteenth-century aquatints, adding nearby Hudson Valley landmarks Olana and Montgomery Place.

LEFT

The gun room, located off of the front vestibule, features a combination of beadboard and smooth walls.

OPPOSITE TOP LEFT

The French doors in the breakfast bay overlook a hidden valley to the north.

OPPOSITE TOP RIGHT

The kitchen backsplash incorporates colorful Moroccan mosaic *zillīg* tile.

OPPOSITE BOTTOM LEFT

A late-eighteenth-century fluted wood mantel carved with Dionysus, grapes, and bucranium (ox skulls) inspired the design of the dining room.

OPPOSITE BOTTOM RIGHT

A coffered alcove in the dining room creates a niche for furniture

DRUMLIN HALL ❖ 207

PROJECTS

MOORE & PENNOYER

Duplex Loft for Isabella Rossellini in the American Thread Building
New York, New York / 1984

Keith Haring Pop Shop
New York, New York / 1986

Keith Haring Studio
New York, New York / 1986

Offices for Interview Magazine
New York, New York / 1988

PENNOYER TURINO ARCHITECTS

Apartment at 520 East 86th Street
New York, New York / 1988

Vico Ristorante
New York, New York / 1988

Hodsoll McKenzie Cloth Store
London, England / 1988

Retail/wholesale shop for a British fabric company including two new shop fronts on Pimlico Road
Stephens, Suzanne. "Currents: In London, Tribute to Soane's Genius." *New York Times*, March 2, 1989.
MacIsaac, Heather Smith. "Classical Fancy." *House & Garden*, November 1989.

Episcopal Mission Society Headquarters
New York, New York / 1988

Townhouse on Perry Street
New York, New York / 1988

Beaverkill Valley Corporation
Lew Beach, New York / 1985–88
Stylebook and design guidelines for development; schematic design for a condominium/detached house project (500 acres)

Allen Stevenson School Faculty Apartments
New York, New York / 1989
Renovation of 12-unit apartment faculty house (8,200 square feet)

Summer House *(unbuilt)*
Southampton, New York / 1989
Design for a house, out buildings, and gardens (9,300 square feet)

PETER PENNOYER ARCHITECTS

The Mark Hotel
New York, New York / 1989
Friends of the Upper East Side Historic Districts Restoration Award, January 11, 1990
Renovation of a 210-room hotel including reconfiguration of all guest rooms, public meeting rooms, restaurant, bar, ballroom, and storefronts (200,000 square feet)
Gordon, Alice. "New York: The Mark." *Elle Decor*, August 1990, p. 40.
Godfrey-June, Jean. "On the Mark." *Contract Design*, December 1990, pp. 40–44.
"The City Hotels—The Mark." *Reports & Great Hotels*, Annual, No. 2, 1990/1991 edition, pp. 44–47.

Andy Warhol Factory/Andy Warhol Foundation for the Visual Arts
New York, New York / 1989
Master plan for the Warhol Factory, offices, and kitchen

Fred Hughes Gallery
New York, New York / 1989

Apartment at 830 Park Avenue
New York, New York / 1989

Storefronts at 963 Lexington Avenue
New York, New York / 1989
Stephens, Suzanne. "Currents: From Mongrelized to Purebred Classic." *New York Times*, July 27, 1989.

East 29th Street Loft
New York, New York / 1990

House for Louis and Adele Auchincloss
Claryville, New York / 1990
"On the Drawing Board: A Roundup of Works in Progress." *Avenue*, vol. 13, no. 4, November 1988.
Auchincloss, Louis. "Wildcat Mountain." *Architectural Digest*, June 1989, pp. 29, 32.
Aronson, Steven M. L. "Arcadian Auchincloss." *Architectural Digest*, August 1992, pp. 102–9.

House on Mishaum Point for Robert and Victoria Pennoyer
South Dartmouth, Massachusetts / 1991
ARCHITECT-IN-CHARGE: Peter Pennoyer
DESIGN DIRECTOR: Gregory Gilmartin
ASSOCIATE-IN-CHARGE: Thomas P. R. Nugent
ASSOCIATES: Daniel Alter, Ashley Hicks
LANDSCAPE DESIGN: Madison Cox Associates, Inc.
INTERIOR DESIGN: Peter Pennoyer
Zevon, Susan. *Inside Architecture: Interiors by Architects*. Rockport, MA: Rockport Publishers, 1997, pp. 184–91.
Stuchin, Marcie, and Susan Abramson. *Waterside Homes*. Glen Cove, NY: PBC International, 1998, pp. 54–57.

Mandarin Oriental Hotel *(unbuilt)*
Hong Kong / 1991
Redesign of public spaces and exterior (40,000 square feet)
ARCHITECT-IN-CHARGE: Peter Pennoyer
DESIGN DIRECTOR: Gregory Gilmartin
ASSOCIATES: Thomas P. R. Nugent, Ashley Hicks, Gil Schafer

House in Cherry Valley for Kent and June Barwick
Cherry Valley, New York / 1991
Renovation and additions
ARCHITECT-IN-CHARGE: Peter Pennoyer

Martha's Vineyard House (*unbuilt*)
Chilmark, Massachusetts / 1991
ARCHITECT-IN-CHARGE: Peter Pennoyer
DESIGN DIRECTOR: Gregory Gilmartin

Katie Ridder Furnishings
944 Lexington Avenue / 1991
ARCHITECT-IN-CHARGE: Peter Pennoyer

Bogardus Hall (*unbuilt*)
Amenia, New York / 1992
Renovation and additions
DESIGN DIRECTOR: Gregory Gilmartin
ASSOCIATES-IN-CHARGE: Kevin Dakin, Gordon Sauer

Apartment at 66 East 79th Street
New York, New York / 1992
ARCHITECT-IN-CHARGE: Peter Pennoyer and Thomas P. R. Nugent
DESIGN DIRECTOR: Gregory Gilmartin
ASSOCIATES: Betty McCaskill, Orlando DeJesus, Hector Griffen
INTERIOR DESIGN: Parish-Hadley Associates

Natori
New York, New York / 1992
Prototype retail store for international lingerie company; boutiques built in Paris and New York
ARCHITECTS-IN-CHARGE: Peter Pennoyer and Thomas P. R. Nugent
INTERIOR DESIGN: Robert Woodfin Jones

Powhatan Plantation
King George, Virginia / 1992
Gazebo and gardens
ARCHITECT-IN-CHARGE: Thomas P. R. Nugent
DESIGN DIRECTOR: Gregory Gilmartin

Beach House
Mantoloking, New Jersey / 1993
ARCHITECT-IN-CHARGE: Peter Pennoyer

ASSOCIATE-IN-CHARGE: Daniel Alter
LANDSCAPE DESIGN: Peter Pennoyer Architects
INTERIOR DESIGN: Alexandra Stoddard, Inc.

Duplex at 37 East 67th Street
New York, York / 1993
ARCHITECT-IN-CHARGE: Thomas P. R. Nugent

Apartment at 1001 Fifth Avenue
New York, New York / 1993
ARCHITECT-IN-CHARGE: Peter Pennoyer
ASSOCIATE: Orlando DeJesus
INTERIOR DESIGN: Katie Ridder, Inc.

Apartment at 907 Fifth Avenue for Count Giovanni Volpi
New York, New York / 1993
ARCHITECT-IN-CHARGE: Peter Pennoyer
INTERIOR DESIGN: Mimi Russell, Inc.

Duplex Penthouse on West 15th Street
New York, New York / 1993
ARCHITECT-IN-CHARGE: Peter Pennoyer
ASSOCIATE: Miriam Cantelmi
LANDSCAPE DESIGN: Madison Cox Associates, Inc.
INTERIOR DESIGN: Peter Pennoyer Architects

Frederick Hughes House
New York, New York / 1993
Restoration of a row house designed by Henry Hardenbergh (4,400 square feet)
ARCHITECT-IN-CHARGE: Peter Pennoyer

The Squirrels (*unbuilt*)
Highland Falls, New York / 1994
Renovation and additions
ARCHITECT-IN-CHARGE: Peter Pennoyer
DESIGN DIRECTOR: Gregory Gilmartin
ASSOCIATE: Daniel Alter

Suites in The Waldorf Towers
New York, New York / 1994
ARCHITECT-IN-CHARGE: Peter Pennoyer
ASSOCIATE-IN-CHARGE: Thomas P. R. Nugent
INTERIOR DESIGN: Owen & Mandolfo, Inc.

Pool House
Greenwich, Connecticut / 1994
ARCHITECTS-IN-CHARGE: Peter Pennoyer and Thomas P. R. Nugent
DESIGN DIRECTOR: Gregory Gilmartin
ASSOCIATE: Chris Spears
INTERIOR DESIGN: Victoria Hagan Interiors

House on Ram Island
Ram Island, New York / 1994
ARCHITECTS-IN-CHARGE: Peter Pennoyer and Thomas P. R. Nugent
DESIGN DIRECTOR: Gregory Gilmartin
ASSOCIATES: Thomas Felton, Gordon Sauer
LANDSCAPE DESIGN: Peter Pennoyer Architects
INTERIOR DESIGN: Carleton Varney of Dorothy Draper & Co.
Kricher, Jill. "Seaside Reverie." *Home Style and Gardening*, February 2000, pp. 64–69.

Apartment at 79 East 79th Street
New York, New York / 1994
ARCHITECTS-IN-CHARGE: Peter Pennoyer and Thomas P. R. Nugent
ASSOCIATES: Nebojsa Savic, Christopher Stoer, Kira Wilson

Townhouse on West 10th Street
New York, New York / 1995
ARCHITECT-IN-CHARGE: Thomas P. R. Nugent
DESIGN DIRECTOR: Gregory Gilmartin
ASSOCIATES: Betty McCaskill, Miriam Cantelmi, Pui Ng, Christopher Stoer, Thomas Felton
LANDSCAPE DESIGN: Madison Cox Associates, Inc.
INTERIOR DESIGN: M. Larsen Interiors
Greco, Stephen. "Perfectly Composed." *Elle Decor*, October/November 1995, pp. 224–31.

Metropolitan Opera Club at Lincoln Center
New York, New York / 1995
Renovation of club rooms within Wallace K. Harrison's Metropolitan Opera House
ARCHITECTS-IN-CHARGE: Peter Pennoyer and Thomas P. R. Nugent

Apartment at 875 Fifth Avenue
New York, New York / 1995
ARCHITECT-IN-CHARGE: Peter Pennoyer
ASSOCIATE: Pui Ng

Blumka Gallery and House
New York, New York / 1996
ARCHITECTS-IN-CHARGE: Thomas P. R. Nugent
DESIGN DIRECTOR: Gregory Gilmartin
ASSOCIATES: Kevin Dakan, Nebojsa Savic, Gordon Sauer, Shaun Jackson, Christopher Stoer, Kira Wilson
LANDSCAPE DESIGN: Madison Cox Associates, Inc.
INTERIOR DESIGN: Peter Pennoyer Architects

East 81st Street Townhouse
New York, New York / 1996
ARCHITECT-IN-CHARGE: Peter Pennoyer
DESIGN DIRECTOR: Gregory Gilmartin
ASSOCIATES: Pui Ng, Nebojsa Savic, Anik Pearson, Miriam Cantelmi
INTERIOR DESIGN: Thomas Jayne Studio, Inc.

House in Mount Kisco
Mount Kisco, New York / 1996
Renovation
ARCHITECT-IN-CHARGE: Peter Pennoyer
ASSOCIATE: Kevin Dakan

Duplex at 941 Park Avenue
New York, New York / 1996
ARCHITECT-IN-CHARGE: Peter Pennoyer
ASSOCIATE-IN-CHARGE: Pui Ng
INTERIOR DESIGN: Thomas Jayne Studio, Inc.

Pennoyer House
Bronxville, New York / 1996
Renovation of a 1920s house
ARCHITECT-IN-CHARGE: Peter Pennoyer
INTERIOR DESIGN: Katie Ridder, Inc.
Owens, Mitchell. "Suburban Dash." *Town & Country*, May 1997, pp. 144–49, 189.
Hunter, Elizabeth H. "Colorful Collaboration." *House Beautiful*, December 1997, pp. 112–19.

Romeo Gigli
New York, New York / 1996
Store design
ARCHITECT-IN-CHARGE: Peter Pennoyer
ASSOCIATE: Kevin Dakan

Fountain House
New York, New York / 1996
Master plan for a clubhouse for the mentally ill, including boardrooms and day rooms (43,800 square feet)
ARCHITECT-IN-CHARGE: Peter Pennoyer and
ASSOCIATED ARCHITECT: Charles Warren Architect

House in Stockbridge (SEE PAGE 208)
Stockbridge, Massachusetts / 1997
ARCHITECT-IN-CHARGE: Peter Pennoyer
DESIGN DIRECTOR: Gregory Gilmartin
ASSOCIATES: Nebojsa Savic, Thomas Felton, Eero Schultz
ASSOCIATED ARCHITECTS: Swanke Hayden Connell Architects
INTERIOR DESIGN: Shaun Jackson Design
LANDSCAPE ARCHITECT: Kelly Varnell Virgona, Inc.

Meadow Lane House (SEE PAGE 164)
Southampton, New York / 1997
ARCHITECT-IN-CHARGE: Peter Pennoyer
DESIGN DIRECTOR: Gregory Gilmartin
ASSOCIATE-IN-CHARGE: Kevin Dakan
ASSOCIATES: Nebojsa Savic, Miriam Cantelmi, Eero Schultz
LANDSCAPE DESIGN: Deborah Nevins Associates
Reed, Julia. "Summer in the Hamptons." *Southern Accents*, May/June 2004, pp. 186–95.

Duplex at River House
New York, New York / 1997
ARCHITECT-IN-CHARGE: Thomas P. R. Nugent
ASSOCIATES: Miriam Cantelmi, Nebojsa Savic
INTERIOR DESIGN: Thomas Jayne Studio, Inc.

House in Florida
Sunset Island II, Florida / 1998
ARCHITECT-IN-CHARGE: Peter Pennoyer
ASSOCIATES: Pui Ng, Nebojsa Savic, Claudia Mulas, Anik Pearson, Elizabeth Graziolo, Kristen Elliott
LANDSCAPE DESIGN: Madison Cox Associates, Inc.
INTERIOR DESIGN: Katie Ridder, Inc.

Orangerie (*unbuilt*)
Bedford, New York / 1998
ARCHITECT-IN-CHARGE: Peter Pennoyer
DESIGN DIRECTOR: Gregory Gilmartin
ASSOCIATE: Anik Pearson
LANDSCAPE DESIGN: Madison Cox Associates, Inc.

New York Stock Exchange Luncheon Club
New York, New York / 1998
Master plan and renovation
ARCHITECT-IN-CHARGE: Peter Pennoyer
INTERIOR DESIGN: Thomas Jayne Studio, Inc.

205 East 63rd Street
New York, New York / 1998
Renovation of public spaces
ARCHITECT-IN-CHARGE: Peter Pennoyer
ASSOCIATE-IN-CHARGE: Pui Ng

Visitors' Center at Van Cortlandt Manor
Croton-on-Hudson, New York / 1999
ARCHITECT-IN-CHARGE: Peter Pennoyer
ASSOCIATES: Pui Ng, Elizabeth Graziolo, Claudia Mulas

Beach House (SEE PAGE 190)
South Dartmouth, Massachusetts / 1999
ARCHITECT-IN-CHARGE: Thomas P. R. Nugent
DESIGN DIRECTOR: Gregory Gilmartin
ASSOCIATES: Nebojsa Savic, Miriam Cantelmi, Christopher Stoer, Claudia Mulas, Eero Schultz
LANDSCAPE ARCHITECT: Kris Horiuchi of Horiuchi & Solien, Inc.
INTERIOR DESIGN: Katie Ridder, Inc.
"New England's New Homes of the Brave." *Country Life*, October 2001, pp. 76–82.
"Classically Styled Residence." *Period Homes*, Spring 2002, pp. 22–30.

Colony Club
New York, New York / 1999
Renovation of the ballroom and other public rooms; master plan
ARCHITECTS-IN-CHARGE: Peter Pennoyer and Thomas P. R. Nugent
DESIGN DIRECTOR: Peter Pennoyer
ASSOCIATES: Nebojsa Savic, Pui Ng, Kevin Dakan, Miriam Cantelmi, Anik Pearson, Elizabeth Graziolo, Christopher Stoer, Claudia Mulas
INTERIOR DESIGN: Thomas Jayne Studio, Inc.

Apartment at 55 Central Park West
New York, New York / 1999
ARCHITECT-IN-CHARGE: Peter Pennoyer
INTERIOR DESIGN: Katie Ridder, Inc.

Model Cottages at The Ford Plantation
Richmond Hill, Georgia / 1999
ARCHITECTS-IN-CHARGE: Peter Pennoyer and Thomas P. R. Nugent
DESIGN DIRECTOR: Anton Glikin
ASSOCIATE: James Taylor
Coleman, David. "Mid-18th-Century Modern: The Classicists Strike Back." *New York Times*, February 10, 2005, House & Home Section.

House in Atlantic Beach (unbuilt)
Atlantic Beach, New York / 1999
ARCHITECT-IN-CHARGE: Peter Pennoyer
DESIGN DIRECTOR: Gregory Gilmartin
ASSOCIATE-IN-CHARGE: Nebojsa Savic
LANDSCAPE DESIGN: Miranda Brooks Landscape Design

Brooke's Bank
Champlain, Virginia / 1999
Renovation and addition, including the replacement of the 1930s wing to a 1751 Georgian house
ARCHITECT-IN-CHARGE: Peter Pennoyer
ASSOCIATE-IN-CHARGE: Nebojsa Savic
ASSOCIATED ARCHITECTS: Douglas Gilpin of Browne, Eighman, Dagleish, Gilpin, Paxton Architects
LANDSCAPE DESIGN: Madison Cox Associates, Inc.
INTERIOR DESIGN: Thomas Jayne Studio, Inc.
Pittel, Christine. "Kitchen of the Month." *House Beautiful*, October 2006, p. 136.

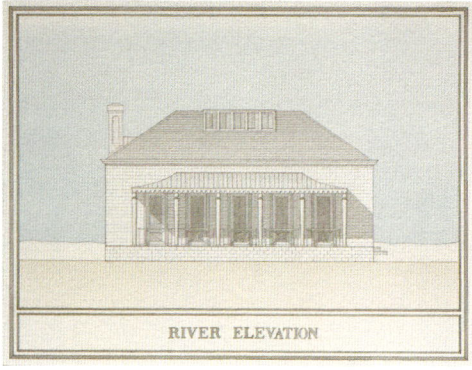

Brooke's Bank Teahouse (unbuilt)
Champlain, Virginia / 1999
ARCHITECT-IN-CHARGE: Peter Pennoyer
ASSOCIATE-IN-CHARGE: Nebojsa Savic
ASSOCIATE: Pui Ng

American Numismatic Society (unbuilt)
New York, New York / 1999
Competition for new headquarters
ARCHITECTS-IN-CHARGE: Peter Pennoyer and Thomas P. R. Nugent

Diamond A Ranch (SEE PAGE 146)
Lincoln County, New Mexico / 1999
ARCHITECT-IN-CHARGE: Peter Pennoyer
DESIGN DIRECTOR: Gregory Gilmartin
ASSOCIATE-IN-CHARGE: Anik Pearson
ASSOCIATES: Nebojsa Savic, Kevin Dakan, Miriam Cantelmi, Claudia Mulas, Christopher Stoer
LANDSCAPE ARCHITECT: Nicholas Quennell and Alison Brawne of Quennell Rothschild & Partners
INTERIOR DESIGN: Thomas Jayne Studio, Inc.
Paul, Linda Leigh. *Ranches of the West*. New York: Rizzoli, 2009, pp. 247–57.

House in New Jersey (unbuilt)
New Vernon, New Jersey / 2000
ARCHITECT-IN-CHARGE: Peter Pennoyer
DESIGN DIRECTOR: Gregory Gilmartin
ASSOCIATE-IN-CHARGE: Nebojsa Savic
ASSOCIATES: Craig Stevens, Anton Glikin, Irina Shumitskaya, James Taylor

San Francisco House (SEE PAGE 118)
El Camino Del Mar, San Francisco, California / 2000
ARCHITECT-IN-CHARGE: Peter Pennoyer
ASSOCIATE-IN-CHARGE: Pui Ng
ASSOCIATES: Elizabeth Graziolo, Diana Gonzalez, Kristen Elliott
LANDSCAPE DESIGN: Madison Cox Associates, Inc.
INTERIOR DESIGN: Katie Ridder, Inc.
Botello, Alfred. "Mediterranean Medley: A Little San Francisco, A lot of Fantasy." *Elle Decor*, August/September 2000, pp. 146–51.

House in Woodside
Woodside, California / 2000
Renovation of a Joseph Esherick house
ARCHITECT-IN-CHARGE: Peter Pennoyer
ASSOCIATES: Pui Ng, Nebojsa Savic, Anik Pearson, Claudia Mulas, Kristen Elliott
INTERIOR DESIGN: Katie Ridder, Inc.
Hunter, Elizabeth H. "Family Ties." *House Beautiful*, September 2001, pp. 118–23.

Tree Tops
Southampton, New York / 2000
Renovation
ARCHITECT-IN-CHARGE: Peter Pennoyer
ASSOCIATES: James Taylor, Anton Glikin, Elizabeth Graziolo
INTERIOR DESIGN: Thomas Jayne Studio, Inc.

Oakley Farm (SEE PAGE 170)
Upperville, Virginia / 2001
ARCHITECTS-IN-CHARGE: Peter Pennoyer and Thomas P. R. Nugent
DESIGN DIRECTOR: Gregory Gilmartin
ASSOCIATE-IN-CHARGE: Nebojsa Savic
ASSOCIATES: Anton Glikin, Pui Ng, Eero Schultz, Elizabeth Graziolo, Andrew Davis, Anthony Goldsby, James Taylor, Kira Wilson
LANDSCAPE DESIGN: Madison Cox Associates, Inc.
INTERIOR DESIGN: Katie Ridder, Inc.
Shaw, Dan. "Grand Revival: A Husband-and-Wife Design Team Restores a Historic but Forlorn Farm in Virginia, Injecting Modern Touches while Remaining True to Its Spirit." *Elle Decor*, October 2005, pp. 222–31.

House in Connecticut
Riverside, Connecticut / 2001
Renovation and additions
ARCHITECT-IN-CHARGE: Peter Pennoyer
DESIGN DIRECTOR: Gregory Gilmartin
ASSOCIATE-IN-CHARGE: Anik Pearson
ASSOCIATES: Nebojsa Savic, Pui Ng, Lavinia Pana, Diana Gonzalez, James Taylor
LANDSCAPE DESIGN: Madison Cox Associates, Inc.
INTERIOR DESIGN: Katie Ridder, Inc.

Guest House
South Dartmouth, Massachusetts / 2002
ARCHITECT-IN-CHARGE: Thomas P. R. Nugent
DESIGN DIRECTOR: Gregory Gilmartin
ASSOCIATES: Nebojsa Savic, Irina Shumitskaya
LANDSCAPE ARCHITECT: Kris Horiuchi of Horiuchi & Solien Landscape Architects

East 73rd Street Townhouse
New York, New York / 2002
ARCHITECT-IN-CHARGE: Thomas P. R. Nugent
DESIGN DIRECTOR: Gregory Gilmartin
ASSOCIATE-IN-CHARGE: Pui Ng
ASSOCIATES: Nebojsa Savic, Lavinia Pana, Anthony Goldsby, Diana Gonzalez, James Taylor, Irina Shumitskaya, Rosette Khorenian, Helmina Kim
INTERIOR DESIGN: Eve Robinson Associates, Inc.

The Church of St. Mary the Virgin
New York, New York / 2002
Renovation projects
ARCHITECT-IN-CHARGE: Peter Pennoyer
ASSOCIATE-IN-CHARGE: Anthony Goldsby
INTERIOR DESIGN: Thomas Jayne Studio, Inc.

Pound Ridge Residence
Pound Ridge, New York / 2002
Renovation and additions
ARCHITECT-IN-CHARGE: Peter Pennoyer
ASSOCIATE-IN-CHARGE: Tiffany Burke
ASSOCIATES: Nebojsa Savic, Craig Stevens, Marc Bailly
INTERIOR DESIGN: Katie Ridder, Inc.

House in Point-O-Woods
Fire Island, New York / 2002
Renovation
ARCHITECT-IN-CHARGE: Peter Pennoyer
ASSOCIATE-IN-CHARGE: James Taylor
ASSOCIATES: Anthony Goldsby, Craig Stevens, Elizabeth Graziolo
INTERIOR DESIGN: Thomas Jayne Studio, Inc.

Henderson, Stephen. "Fire Island Idyll." *House Beautiful*, April 2003, pp. 74–83.

Polo Field and Design for Equestrian Facility (unbuilt)
Water Mill, New York / 2002
ARCHITECT-IN-CHARGE: Peter Pennoyer
ASSOCIATE-IN-CHARGE: James Taylor
ASSOCIATES: Anton Glikin, Rosette Khorenian
LANDSCAPE ARCHITECT: Nicholas Quennell and Mark Bunnell of Quennell Rothschild & Partners
EQUESTRIAN FACILITIES CONSULTANT: Robert Jolicoeur of International Equestrian Design

The Knickerbocker Club
New York, New York / 1998–2004
Roof terrace restaurant; renovation projects
ARCHITECTS-IN-CHARGE: Peter Pennoyer and Thomas P. R. Nugent
ASSOCIATES: James Taylor, Mark Herring, Elizabeth Graziolo

Coaching Club
New York, New York / 2003
Renovation
ARCHITECT-IN-CHARGE: Peter Pennoyer
ASSOCIATES: James Taylor, Mark Herring, Elizabeth Graziolo

The Breakers (study)
Newport, Rhode Island / 2003
Feasibility study for visitors' center
ARCHITECT-IN-CHARGE: Peter Pennoyer
ASSOCIATE-IN-CHARGE: Irina Shumitskaya

House on Gracie Lane (unbuilt)
Easthampton, New York / 2003
ARCHITECT-IN-CHARGE: Peter Pennoyer
DESIGN DIRECTOR: Gregory Gilmartin
ASSOCIATE: Kathleen Wiberg

House in Carmel Valley (unbuilt)
Santa Lucia Preserve, Carmel Valley, California / 2003
ARCHITECT-IN-CHARGE: Peter Pennoyer
ASSOCIATES: Nebojsa Savic, Kristen Haller
LANDSCAPE DESIGN: Suzman Design Associates
INTERIOR DESIGN: Beverly Ellsley Design

House in Germantown (unbuilt)
Germantown, New York / 2003
ARCHITECT-IN-CHARGE: Peter Pennoyer
ASSOCIATE-IN-CHARGE: Irina Shumitskaya

Mountain House
The Colony at White Pine Canyon, Summit County, Utah / 2003
ARCHITECT-IN-CHARGE: Peter Pennoyer
ASSOCIATE-IN-CHARGE: Anik Pearson
ASSOCIATES: Anton Glikin, Nebojsa Savic, Rosette Khorenian
LANDSCAPE ARCHITECT: Jack Johnson Co.
INTERIOR DESIGN: Karyn Bloom

Apartment at 1125 Fifth Avenue
New York, New York / 2003
ARCHITECT-IN-CHARGE: Peter Pennoyer
ASSOCIATE-IN-CHARGE: Mark Herring
ASSOCIATES: Andrew Davis, Tiffany Burke, Kathleen Wiberg
INTERIOR DESIGN: Eric Cohler Design

Apartment in The Dakota
New York, New York / 2003
ARCHITECT-IN-CHARGE: Peter Pennoyer
ASSOCIATE-IN-CHARGE: Mark Herring
ASSOCIATES: Andrew Davis, Hayley Chow Moreno, Tiffany Burke

INTERIOR DESIGN: Bilhuber & Associates
Vail, Amanda. "Inner Space." *Town & Country*, October 2004, pp. 244–50.

Adirondack Camp
Bay Pond Park, Paul Smith's, New York / 2003
ARCHITECT-IN-CHARGE: Peter Pennoyer
DESIGN DIRECTOR: Gregory Gilmartin
ASSOCIATE-IN-CHARGE: James Taylor
ASSOCIATES: Nebojsa Savic, Pui Ng, Anik Pearson, Irina Shumitskaya
LANDSCAPE ARCHITECT: Reed Hilderbrand Associates, Inc.
INTERIOR DESIGN: Evergreen Interiors

Apartment on Gracie Square
New York, New York / 2004
ARCHITECT-IN-CHARGE: Peter Pennoyer
DESIGN DIRECTOR: Anton Glikin
ASSOCIATE-IN-CHARGE: Mark Herring
ASSOCIATE: Hayley Chow Moreno
INTERIOR DESIGN: Katie Ridder, Inc.

Apartment at 131 East 69th Street
New York, New York / 2004
ARCHITECT-IN-CHARGE: Peter Pennoyer
ASSOCIATE-IN-CHARGE: Hayley Chow Moreno
ASSOCIATE: Andrew Davis
INTERIOR DESIGN: Thomas Jayne Studio, Inc.

Adirondack Camp (SEE PAGE 128)
Paul Smith's, New York / 2004
ARCHITECT-IN-CHARGE: Peter Pennoyer
ASSOCIATE-IN-CHARGE: James Taylor
ASSOCIATES: Anton Glikin, Nebojsa Savic, Irina Shumitskaya, Craig Stevens, Marc Bailly, Anthony Goldsby

LANDSCAPE ARCHITECT: Alec Gunn of Gunn Landscape Architects, Inc.
INTERIOR DESIGN: Evergreen House Interiors

Townhouse on East 69th Street
New York, New York / 2004
Preservation study
ASSOCIATE-IN-CHARGE: Andrew Davis

Limestone Mansion (SEE PAGE 90)
New York, New York / 2004
ARCHITECT-IN-CHARGE: Peter Pennoyer
DESIGN DIRECTOR: Gregory Gilmartin
ASSOCIATES: Anton Glikin, Nebojsa Savic, Pui Ng, Craig Stevens, Miriam Cantelmi, Lavinia Pana, Kristen Elliott, Kira Wilson, Claudia Mulas, Anthony Goldsby, Diana Gonzalez, Kathleen Wiberg, Helmina Kim
ASSOCIATED ARCHITECTS: Swanke Hayden Connell Architects
ARCHITECTURAL CONSULTANT: Theodore H. M. Prudon of Prudon & Partners LLP
INTERIOR DESIGN: Shaun Jackson Design

Apartment at 1030 Fifth Avenue
New York, New York / 2004
ARCHITECT-IN-CHARGE: Peter Pennoyer
ASSOCIATES: Mark Herring, Anton Glikin, Andrew Davis
INTERIOR DESIGN: Katie Ridder, Inc.
Rhodes, Melissa Barrett. "Clearing the Way." *Elle Decor*, March 2006, pp. 142–49.

Federal Reserve Bank of New York (unbuilt)
New York, New York / 2005
Competition for the renovation of reception rooms
ARCHITECT-IN-CHARGE: Peter Pennoyer
ASSOCIATES: Craig Doyle, Timothy P. Kelly

Turtle Creek House (unbuilt)
Dallas, Texas / 2005
ARCHITECT-IN-CHARGE: Peter Pennoyer
DESIGN DIRECTOR: Gregory Gilmartin
ASSOCIATE-IN-CHARGE: Craig Stevens
ASSOCIATES: Nebojsa Savic, Andrew Davis, Anton Glikin, Eero Schultz, James Taylor

Lenox Hill Townhouse (SEE PAGE 80)
New York, New York / 2005
ARCHITECTS-IN-CHARGE: Peter Pennoyer and Thomas P. R. Nugent
DESIGN DIRECTOR: Gregory Gilmartin
ASSOCIATE-IN-CHARGE: Pui Ng
ASSOCIATES: Nebojsa Savic, Anton Glikin, Irina Shumitskaya, Craig Stevens, Tiffany Burke, Kristen Haller
INTERIOR DESIGN: Victoria Hagan Interiors
"Design Notebook: Rooms of Their Own." *Architectural Digest,* December 2007, p. 79.
Cochran, Samuel. "American Revival." *Elle Decor,* May 2009, pp. 125–31.

Apartment on Gracie Square
New York, New York / 2005
ARCHITECT-IN-CHARGE: Elizabeth Graziolo
DESIGN DIRECTOR: Anton Glikin
ASSOCIATE: Mark Herring
INTERIOR DESIGN: Christie Hansen Interior Design

House on Penobscot Bay
(SEE PAGE 136)
Penobscot Bay, Maine / 2005
ARCHITECT-IN-CHARGE: Peter Pennoyer
DESIGN DIRECTOR: Gregory Gilmartin
ASSOCIATE-IN-CHARGE: James Taylor
ASSOCIATES: Irina Shumitskaya, Elizabeth Graziolo, Anik Pearson, Nebojsa Savic, Lavinia Pana
LANDSCAPE ARCHITECT: Reed Hilderbrand Associates, Inc.
INTERIOR DESIGN: Thomas Jayne Studio, Inc.

Beaux-Arts Townhouse
(SEE PAGE 72)
New York, New York / 2005
ARCHITECTS-IN-CHARGE: Peter Pennoyer and Thomas P. R. Nugent
DESIGN DIRECTOR: Gregory Gilmartin
ASSOCIATE-IN-CHARGE: Craig Stevens
ASSOCIATES: Nebojsa Savic, Pui Ng, Anton Glikin, Eero Schultz, Elizabeth Graziolo, Irina Shumitskaya, Jennifer Smith, Stephanie Lo, Andrew Davis, Marc Bailly, Anthony Goldsby
LANDSCAPE DESIGN: Peter Pennoyer Architects
INTERIOR DESIGN: Kirsten Kelli, LLC
Gray, Christopher. "Streetscapes: East 77th Street, An Upper East Side Block Offers a Panoply of Styles." *New York Times,* May 16, 2004.
Capelin, Joan. "Premises, Premises." *Oculus,* Spring 2008.
Nasatir, Judith. "Twice as Stylish: Upper East Side Townhouse." *Veranda,* April 2010, pp. 106–15.

House and Guest House in St. Bart's
(unbuilt)
Saint Barthélemy, French West Indies / 2005
ARCHITECT-IN-CHARGE: Peter Pennoyer
ASSOCIATE-IN-CHARGE: Julio Gavilanes
ASSOCIATE: Daniel McPherson

Pool House (unbuilt)
Penobscot Bay, Maine / 2006
ARCHITECTS-IN-CHARGE: Peter Pennoyer and Elizabeth Graziolo
ASSOCIATE-IN-CHARGE: Craig Doyle
ASSOCIATES: Timothy P. Kelly, Lucas Hafeli, Silvia L. Mohan, Stephanie Lo
LANDSCAPE ARCHITECT: Nicholas Pouder of Pouder Design Group

West Side Rail Yards (unbuilt)
New York, New York / 2006
Scheme for public square elevated above bus access lanes and framed by a screen of classical architecture
ASSOCIATE-IN-CHARGE: Anton Glikin
Magnet, Myron. "Reimagining the Far West Side." *City Journal,* Autumn 2004, pp. 64–77.

East 38th Street Apartment
New York, New York / 2006
ARCHITECT-IN-CHARGE: Peter Pennoyer
ASSOCIATE-IN-CHARGE: Mark Herring
ASSOCIATES: Timothy P. Kelly, Craig Stevens, Andrew Davis
INTERIOR DESIGN: Bilhuber & Associates

East Side Duplex (SEE PAGE 38)
New York, New York / 2006
DESIGN DIRECTOR: Anton Glikin
ASSOCIATE-IN-CHARGE: Mark Herring
ASSOCIATES: Todd M. Brickell, Anton Glikin, F. Patrick Mohan, Silvia L. Mohan, Timothy P. Kelly, Neha Wallia
INTERIOR DESIGN: Eve Robinson Associates, Inc.

Apartment at 1165 Fifth Avenue
New York, New York / 2006
ARCHITECT-IN-CHARGE: Elizabeth Graziolo
ASSOCIATES: Mark Herring, Stephanie Lo
INTERIOR DESIGN: Katie Ridder, Inc.
Owens, Mitchell. "Step Lively." *Elle Decor*, March 2008, pp. 146–51.

Fordune
Southampton, New York / 2006
Renovation and additions
ARCHITECT-IN-CHARGE: Peter Pennoyer
ASSOCIATE-IN-CHARGE: Kathleen Wiberg
ASSOCIATES: Meredith Thomson, Eero Schultz, Stephanie Lo, James Taylor, Kristen Haller
LANDSCAPE ARCHITECT: Edmund D. Hollander of Edmund Hollander Landscape Architects
INTERIOR DESIGN: Matthew Patrick Smyth Interior Design

House in the Santa Lucia Range
(SEE PAGE 156)
Carmel Valley, California / 2006
ARCHITECT-IN-CHARGE: Peter Pennoyer
ASSOCIATE-IN-CHARGE: Nebojsa Savic
ASSOCIATES: Kristen Haller, Tiffany Burke, Andrew Davis
LANDSCAPE DESIGN: Suzman Design Associates
INTERIOR DESIGN: Paul Wiseman of The Wiseman Group Interior Design, Inc.

House on Skellenger Lane (unbuilt)
Napa, California / 2006
ARCHITECT-IN-CHARGE: Peter Pennoyer
ASSOCIATE-IN-CHARGE: Kristen Haller
ASSOCIATES: Nebojsa Savic, F. Patrick Mohan, Meredith Thomson
LANDSCAPE DESIGN: Madison Cox Associates, Inc.

Triplex Apartment at 655 Park Avenue (unbuilt)
New York, New York / 2006
ARCHITECT-IN-CHARGE: Peter Pennoyer
ASSOCIATES: Timothy P. Kelly, Julio Gavilanes
INTERIOR DESIGN: Jacques Grange Interiors

House on West 12th Street (unbuilt)
New York, New York / 2007
ARCHITECT-IN-CHARGE: Peter Pennoyer
ASSOCIATE-IN-CHARGE: Craig Doyle
ASSOCIATES: Lisa Lombardi, Graham Ivory

House on the Bay (unbuilt)
Virginia Beach, Virginia / 2007
ARCHITECT-IN-CHARGE: Peter Pennoyer
DESIGN DIRECTOR: Gregory Gilmartin
ASSOCIATE-IN-CHARGE: Hayley Chow Moreno
ASSOCIATES: Sean Blackwell, Silvia L. Mohan, Julio Gavilanes

Pennoyer House
Bronxville, New York / 2007
Renovation of a 1920s Charles Lewis Bowman house
ARCHITECT-IN-CHARGE: Peter Pennoyer
INTERIOR: Katie Ridder, Inc.
Abramovitch, Ingrid. "Match Game." *Elle Decor*, July/August 2008, pp. 114–21.

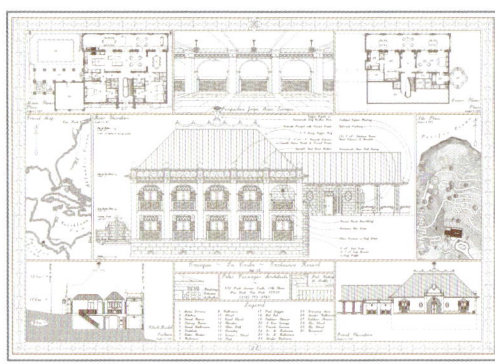

Cacique Resort (unbuilt)
Guanacaste, Costa Rica / 2007
Competition for island resort villas
ARCHITECT-IN-CHARGE: Peter Pennoyer
ASSOCIATE-IN-CHARGE: Oscar A. Carrera

House on Maple Street
San Francisco, California / 2007
ARCHITECT-IN-CHARGE: Peter Pennoyer
ASSOCIATE-IN-CHARGE: Kristen Haller
ASSOCIATES: Meredith Thomson, Daniel McPherson
INTERIOR DESIGN: Bilhuber & Associates
Bilhuber, Jeffrey. *Defining Luxury: The Qualities of Life at Home*. New York: Rizzoli, 2008.

Fifth Avenue Triplex
(SEE PAGE 30)
New York, New York / 2007
ARCHITECT-IN-CHARGE: Peter Pennoyer
DESIGN DIRECTOR: Gregory Gilmartin
ASSOCIATE-IN-CHARGE: Hayley Chow Moreno
ASSOCIATES: Nebojsa Savic, Andrew Davis, Pui Ng, Eero Schultz, Floriane Gremion, Anton Glikin, Elizabeth Graziolo
INTERIOR DESIGN: Katie Leede, Digs by Katie

Brae Burn Country Club (unbuilt)
Westchester, New York / 2008
Competition
ARCHITECT-IN-CHARGE: Peter Pennoyer
ASSOCIATE-IN-CHARGE: Craig Doyle

Dunwalke (unbuilt)
Bedminster, New Jersey / 2008
Master plan; renovation of Cross & Cross-designed house; new squash building; landscape design
ARCHITECT-IN-CHARGE: Peter Pennoyer
DESIGN DIRECTOR: Gregory Gilmartin
ASSOCIATE-IN-CHARGE: Nebojsa Savic
ASSOCIATES: Anton Glikin, F. Patrick Mohan, Sean Blackwell, Craig Doyle, Benjamin Sirota

House in Peapack (unbuilt)
Peapack, New Jersey / 2008
Compound including farm buildings and guest cottage
ARCHITECT-IN-CHARGE: Peter Pennoyer
DESIGN DIRECTOR: Anton Glikin
ASSOCIATE-IN-CHARGE: Nebojsa Savic
ASSOCIATES: Anton Glikin, F. Patrick Mohan, Sean Blackwell, Aaron Rigby, Benjamin Sirota, Francine Hsu Davis, Jennifer Gerakaris
LANDSCAPE DESIGN: Peter Cummin of Cummin Associates, Inc.

Carnegie Hill Brownstone (SEE PAGE 64)
New York, New York / 2008
ARCHITECT-IN-CHARGE: Peter Pennoyer
DESIGN DIRECTOR: Eero Schultz
ASSOCIATE-IN-CHARGE: Francine Hsu Davis
ASSOCIATES: Nebojsa Savic, Silvia L. Mohan, Sean Blackwell, Craig Stevens, Hayley Chow Moreno, Drew Davis, Kathleen Wiberg
LANDSCAPE ARCHITECT: Maureen Hackett of Hackett Landscape Design, Inc.
INTERIOR DESIGN: Matthew Patrick Smyth Interior Design

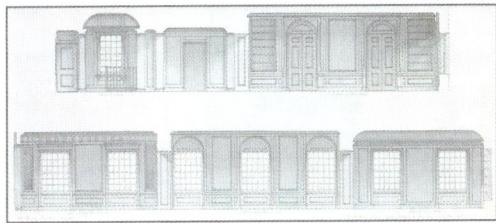

The Hotchkiss School, Paul Nitze Center for Global Understanding and Independent Thinking
Lakeville, Connecticut / 2008
Renovation to interior of Delano & Aldrich's Monahan Gymnasium
ARCHITECT-IN-CHARGE: Nebojsa Savic
DESIGN DIRECTOR: Anton Glikin
ASSOCIATES: Benjamin Sirota, Sean Blackwell
EXECUTIVE ARCHITECTS: Butler Rogers Baskett Architects
INTERIOR DESIGN: Carolyn Griffith

East 64th Street Townhouse
New York, New York / 2008
ASSOCIATE-IN-CHARGE: Mark Herring
ASSOCIATES: Timothy P. Kelly, Todd M. Brickell
INTERIOR DESIGN: Bilhuber & Associates
LANDSCAPE ARCHITECT: Amber Fredz

Upper East Side Townhouse (SEE PAGE 100)
New York, New York / 2008
ARCHITECT-IN-CHARGE: Thomas P. R. Nugent
ASSOCIATE-IN-CHARGE: Julio Gavilanes
ASSOCIATES: Timothy P. Kelly, Anton Glikin, F. Patrick Mohan
LANDSCAPE DESIGN: Madison Cox Associates, Inc.
INTERIOR DESIGN: Bilhuber & Associates

Park Avenue Apartment (SEE PAGE 46)
New York, New York / 2008

ARCHITECT-IN-CHARGE: Peter Pennoyer
DESIGN DIRECTOR: Anton Glikin
ASSOCIATE-IN-CHARGE: Pui Ng
ASSOCIATES: Nebojsa Savic, F. Patrick Mohan, Timothy P. Kelly, Sean Blackwell, Meredith Thomson, Daniel McPherson
INTERIOR DESIGN: David Kleinberg Design Associates

House on Oyster Bay (unbuilt)
Centre Island, New York / 2008
ARCHITECT-IN-CHARGE: Peter Pennoyer
DESIGN DIRECTOR: Gregory Gilmartin
ASSOCIATE-IN-CHARGE: Jennifer Gerakaris
ASSOCIATES: Anton Glikin, Timothy P. Kelly, Lucas Hafeli, F. Patrick Mohan, Cory Roffelsen, Sean Blackwell, Francine Hsu Davis, Hayley Chow Moreno

East 75th Street Townhouse (unbuilt)
New York, New York / 2008
ARCHITECT-IN-CHARGE: Peter Pennoyer
DESIGN DIRECTOR: Gregory Gilmartin
ASSOCIATE-IN-CHARGE: Jennifer Gerakaris
ASSOCIATES: Timothy P. Kelly, Anton Glikin, Cory Roffelsen, Craig Doyle, Stephen Piersanti, Daniel McPherson, Francine Hsu Davis
INTERIOR DESIGN: Thomas Jayne Studio, Inc.

Apartment at The Plaza
New York, New York / 2009
ARCHITECT-IN-CHARGE: Peter Pennoyer
DESIGN DIRECTOR: Anton Glikin
ASSOCIATE-IN-CHARGE: Cecilia Rogers
ASSOCIATE: Stephen Piersanti
INTERIOR DESIGN: Katie Ridder, Inc.

Federal House (SEE PAGE 180)
New England / 2009
ARCHITECTS-IN-CHARGE: Peter Pennoyer and Elizabeth Graziolo
DESIGN DIRECTOR: Gregory Gilmartin
ASSOCIATE-IN-CHARGE: Kathleen Wiberg
ASSOCIATES: Nebojsa Savic, Todd M. Brickell, Anton Glikin, Silvia L. Mohan, Aaron Rigby, Mark Herring, Lucas Hafeli, F. Patrick Mohan, Andrew Davis, Daniel McPherson, Graham Ivory, Joshua Coleman
LANDSCAPE DESIGN: Saltair

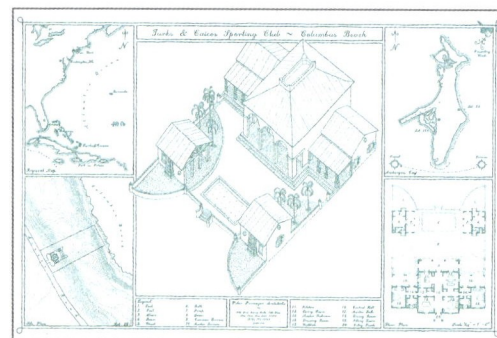

Two Island Houses (*unbuilt*)
Turks and Caicos Islands, British West Indies / 2009
ARCHITECT-IN-CHARGE: Peter Pennoyer
ASSOCIATE-IN-CHARGE: Oscar A. Carrera

Grosvenor Atterbury Townhouse
(SEE PAGE 108)
New York, New York / 2009
ARCHITECT-IN-CHARGE: Elizabeth Graziolo
DESIGN DIRECTOR: Gregory Gilmartin
ASSOCIATES: Cecilia Rodgers, Thomas Lamontagne, F. Patrick Mohan, Silvia L. Mohan, Stephanie Lo, Stephen Piersanti, Aaron Rigby, Benjamin Sirota, Dana Laudani, Diana Reising, Joshua Coleman
FACADE CONSULTANT: Richard Pieper, Jan Hird Pokorny Associates, Inc.
LANDSCAPE DESIGN: Jane Gil of Horticulture, LLC
INTERIOR DESIGN: Christie Hansen Interior Design

Monument for the Irish Green, University of Notre Dame (*unbuilt*)
Notre Dame, Indiana / 2009
Competition
DESIGN DIRECTOR: Anton Glikin
ASSOCIATE-IN-CHARGE: Timothy P. Kelly

House in Amagansett
Amagansett, New York / 2009
Renovation to house; new guest house, pool house, yoga studio, pool pavilion, and tennis pavilion
ARCHITECT-IN-CHARGE: Peter Pennoyer
DESIGN DIRECTOR: Mark Herring
ASSOCIATE-IN-CHARGE: Pui Ng
ASSOCIATES: Todd M. Brickell, Craig Doyle, Oscar A. Carrera, Sean Blackwell, Aaron Rigby, Benjamin Sirota

LANDSCAPE ARCHITECT: Edmund D. Hollander of Edmund Hollander Landscape Architects
LANDSCAPE DESIGN: Miranda Brooks Landscape Design
INTERIOR DESIGN: Jacques Grange Interiors

House on Cypress Point
Pebble Beach, California / 2009
ARCHITECT-IN-CHARGE: Peter Pennoyer
ASSOCIATE-IN-CHARGE: Kristen Haller
ASSOCIATE: Cleary Shea
INTERIOR DESIGN: Katie Ridder, Inc.
Gross, Jaimie. "Point of Departure." *Town & Country*, May 2010, pp. 126–131 & 145.

Drumlin Hall (SEE PAGE 196)
Pine Plains, New York / 2009
ARCHITECTS-IN-CHARGE: Thomas P. R. Nugent and Peter Pennoyer
DESIGN DIRECTOR: Gregory Gilmartin
ASSOCIATES: Nebojsa Savic, Anton Glikin, Sean Blackwell, Timothy P. Kelly, F. Patrick Mohan, Eero Schultz, Andrew Davis, James Taylor
LANDSCAPE DESIGN: Ruthie Bontecou of RB Ltd.
INTERIOR DESIGN: Thomas Jayne Studio, Inc.
Ruhling, Nancy. "Classical Language: A Palladian-inspired villa rises in the Hudson Valley." *Period Homes*, May 2010, pp. 10–13.

East River Apartment (SEE PAGE 54)
New York, New York / 2009
DESIGN DIRECTOR AND ASSOCIATE-IN-CHARGE: Mark Herring

ASSOCIATES: Oscar A. Carrera, Todd M. Brickell
INTERIOR DESIGN: Michael S. Smith, Inc.
LIGHTING DESIGN: Cline, Bettridge, Berntstein Lighting Design, Inc.

Pavilion Peterhof
Peter Pennoyer Architects, New York / 2009
1/12 scale model of a folly
DESIGN DIRECTOR: Anton Glikin
PLASTERWORK: Balmer Architectural Mouldings, Ltd.

The Regional History Center, Historic Hudson Valley
Mount Pleasant, New York / 2010
ARCHITECT-IN-CHARGE: Peter Pennoyer
ASSOCIATE-IN-CHARGE: Nebojsa Savic
ASSOCIATES: F. Patrick Mohan, Gregory Gilmartin, Thomas P. E. Nugent, Oscar A. Carrera, Silvia L. Mohan, Cecilia Rodgers, John Gibbons, Hayley Chow Moreno, Stephen Piersanti, Dana Laudani
CIVIL ENGINEER/LANDSCAPE ARCHITECT: Andrew Tung of Divney Tung Schwalbe, LLP
INTERIOR DESIGN: Thomas Jayne Studio, Inc.

Apartment at 812 Park Avenue
New York, New York / 2010
ARCHITECT-IN-CHARGE: Peter Pennoyer
ASSOCIATE-IN-CHARGE: Mark Herring
ASSOCIATES: Todd M. Brickell, Oscar A. Carrera, Lucas Hafeli, John Gibbons, Cecilia Rodgers, Cleary Shea, Cory Roffelsen
INTERIOR DESIGN: Barbara Lazrus, Royce Kilbourn

Apartment at 1070 Park Avenue
New York, New York / 2010
ARCHITECT-IN-CHARGE: Peter Pennoyer
DESIGN DIRECTOR AND ASSOCIATE-IN-CHARGE: Mark Herring
ASSOCIATES: Oscar A. Carerra, Todd M. Brickell, Lucas Hafeli
INTERIOR DESIGN: Thomas Jayne Studio, Inc.

Apartment at One Beekman Place
New York, New York / 2010
ARCHITECT-IN-CHARGE: Peter Pennoyer
ASSOCIATE-IN-CHARGE: Pui Ng
ASSOCIATES: Cory Roffelsen, Lucas Hafeli, F. Patrick Mohan, John Gibbons, Cecilia Rodgers
INTERIOR DESIGN: Victoria Hagan Interiors

House in Darien
Darien, Connecticut / 2010
Renovation to a 1908 house
ARCHITECT-IN-CHARGE: Thomas P. R. Nugent
ASSOCIATES: Boaz M. Golani, F. Patrick Mohan, Cecilia Rodgers
INTERIOR DESIGN: Katie Ridder, Inc.

New York Genealogical & Biographical Society
New York, New York / 2010
New offices and library in the Bar Building
ARCHITECT-IN-CHARGE: Thomas P. R. Nugent
DESIGN: John Claflin
ASSOCIATES: Nebojsa Savic, Sean Blackwell, Silvia L. Mohan

923 Fifth Avenue
New York, New York / 2010
ASSOCIATE-IN-CHARGE: Mark Herring
ASSOCIATES: Todd M. Brickell, Oscar A. Carrera, Lucas Hafeli, John Gibbons
INTERIOR DESIGN: Matthew Patrick Smyth Interior Design

Owl House
Bronxville, New York / In progress
Renovation and addition to 1896 William W. Kent house
ARCHITECT-IN-CHARGE: Elizabeth Graziolo
DESIGN DIRECTOR: Gregory Gilmartin
ASSOCIATE-IN-CHARGE: Timothy P. Kelly
ASSOCIATES: Thomas Lamontagne, Cleary Shea, Lucas Hafeli, Joseph Pagac, Silvia L. Mohan, Anton Glikin, Cory Roffelsen, Jennifer Gerakaris
INTERIOR DESIGN: Katie Ridder, Inc.
LANDSCAPE DESIGN: Memrie Lewis Landscape Design, LLC with Saint-Amand Landscape Design, LLC

House in Rye
Westchester County, New York / In progress
Renovation and additions to a 1904 house
ARCHITECT-IN-CHARGE: Peter Pennoyer
DESIGN DIRECTOR: Anton Glikin
ASSOCIATE-IN-CHARGE: Catherine Popple
ASSOCIATES: Kathleen Donovan, Silvia L. Mohan, Lucas Hafeli, F. Patrick Mohan, Cecilia Rodgers, John Gibbons, Timothy P. Kelly
LANDSCAPE ARCHITECT: Sean Jancski of Inviting Environments
INTERIOR DESIGN: Paul Latham

House on Georgica Pond
East Hampton, New York / In progress
ARCHITECT-IN-CHARGE: Peter Pennoyer
ASSOCIATE-IN-CHARGE: Jennifer Gerakaris
ASSOCIATES: Nebojsa Savic, Lucas Hafeli, Cecilia Rodgers, F. Patrick Mohan, Pui Ng
LANDSCAPE DESIGN: Edwina von Gail
INTERIOR DESIGN: Matthew Patrick Smyth Interior Design

Townhouse on East 75th Street
New York, New York / In progress
ARCHITECT-IN-CHARGE: Peter Pennoyer
DESIGN DIRECTOR: Anton Glikin
ASSOCIATE-IN-CHARGE: Jennifer Gerakaris
ASSOCIATES: Cecilia Rodgers, Mark Herring, Lucas Hafeli, Cory Roffelsen
INTERIOR DESIGN: Jacques Grange Interiors

House in Maine
In progress
ARCHITECT-IN-CHARGE: Peter Pennoyer
DESIGN DIRECTOR: Gregory Gilmartin
ASSOCIATE-IN-CHARGE: James Taylor
ASSOCIATES: Nebojsa Savic, John Gibbons, Lucas Hafeli, F. Patrick Mohan, Timothy P. Kelly, Cecilia Rodgers, Cleary Shea, Jennifer Gerakaris
LANDSCAPE ARCHITECT: Stephen Mohr of Mohr & Seredin Landscape Architects, Inc.

Townhouse on East 80th Street
New York, New York / In progress
ARCHITECTS-IN-CHARGE: Peter Pennoyer and Elizabeth Graziolo
DESIGN DIRECTOR: Gregory Gilmartin
ASSOCIATES: Cleary Shea, Nebojsa Savic, Timothy P. Kelly, Elizabeth Graziolo, F. Patrick Mohan, Cecilia Rodgers, Cory Roffelsen

Bank Street Townhouse
New York, New York / In progress
ARCHITECTS-IN-CHARGE: Thomas P. R. Nugent and Peter Pennoyer
DESIGN DIRECTOR: Gregory Gilmartin
ASSOCIATES: Joseph Pagac, Thomas Lamontagne, Cleary Shea, Cecilia Rodgers, Mark Herring

PHOTO AND DRAWING CREDITS

Peter Aaron: 12, 26, 146–55 Diamond A Ranch
Luca Allen: 218 Apartment at 1165 Fifth Avenue
Paul Barker: 190–95 Beach House
Philip Beaurline: 214 Brooke's Bank
James Bleecker: 221 New York Genealogical & Biographical Society
Oscar A. Carrera: 218 Cacique Resort, 220 Two Island Houses, 221 Apartment at 812 Park Avenue
Langdon Clay: 24, 210 House for Louis and Adele Auchincloss
Craig Doyle: 217 Pool House
Robert Drake: 209 Hodsoll McKenzie Cloth Store
Scott Frances: 4–5, 6–7, 17, 18–19, 23 right, 28–29, 30–37 Fifth Avenue Triplex, 38–45 East Side Duplex, 54–61 East River Apartment, 62–63, 64–71 Carnegie Hill Brownstone, 80–89 Lenox Hill Townhouse, 108–17 Grosvenor Atterbury Townhouse, 118–25 San Francisco House, 170–79 Oakley Farm, 212 Blumka Gallery and East 81st Street Townhouse, 214 House in Woodside, 215 East 73rd Street Townhouse, 216 Apartment at 1125 Fifth Avenue and Apartment on Gracie Square, 219 East 64th Street Townhouse
Anton Glikin: 13, 23 bottom, 27 left, 93 bottom right, 95 top left, 182 top right, 213 Orangerie and Model Cottages at Ford Plantation, 214 House in New Jersey, 217 Turtle Creek House and West Side Rail Yards, 219 House in Peapack, The Hotchkiss School, and House on Oyster Bay, 220 Monument for the Irish Green, 221 Owl House, 222 House in Rye, 223 grille drawing, endpapers
Mick Hales: 21, 209 Apartment at 520 East 86th Street and Townhouse on Perry Street, 210 Storefronts at 963 Lexington Avenue, 211 Apartment at 66 East 79th Street and Beach House, 212 Pool House and Townhouse on West 10th Street
Reto Halme: 164–69 Meadow Lane House
Sung Hung: 210 Mandarin Oriental Hotel
Andre Junget: 219 East 75th Street Townhouse
Timothy P. Kelly: 25 right, 33 plan, 35 north elevation, 41 plan, 48 plan, 57 plan, 66 plan, 67 section, 70 top left, 74 plan and section, 82 section, 84 plan, 106 plan, 108, 112 plan and section, 114 top left, 120 plan, 130 plan, 139 plan, 141 section, 144 section, 160 plan, 174 section, 176 plan, 182 top left, 185 plan, 193 plan, 194 section, 198 plan, 199 section, 203 bottom left, 217 Federal Reserve Bank of New York
Christopher Mason: 46–53 Park Avenue Apartment
Matthew Millman: 20, 156–163 House in the Santa Lucia Range
F. Patrick Mohan: 103 top left, 218 House on the Bay, 221 The Regional History Center
Peter Paige: 210 The Mark Hotel
Peter Pennoyer: 211 Powhatan Plantation, 218 House on Maple Street, 220 House in Amagansett
Peter Pennoyer Architects: 155 plan, 168 plan
Jahn Peterson: 22, 209 Keith Haring Pop Shop and Studio
Eric Piasecki: 2–3, 100–7 Upper East Side Townhouse, 220 House on Cypress Point
Nebojsa Savic: 212 House on Ram Island, 214 Brooke's Bank Teahouse
Eero Schultz: 70 top right
Irina Shumitskaya: 129, 143 top left, 216 House in Germantown
Brian Vanden Brink: 180–89 Federal House
Jonathan Wallen: 1, 8–9, 10–11, 14, 15, 27 right, 72–79 Beaux-Arts Townhouse, 90–99 Limestone Mansion, 126–127, 128–35 Adirondack Camp, 136–45 House on Penobscot Bay, 196–207 Drumlin Hall, 208, 215 House in Connecticut and House in Point-O-Woods, 216 Townhouse on 11 East 69th Street, 221 Pavilion Peterhof
Wade Zimmerman: 25 left, 210 House on Mishaum Point

ACKNOWLEDGMENTS

THE PAGES OF THIS BOOK REFLECT THE CONTRIBUTIONS OF SO MANY, not only those responsible for creating and designing what is inside but also everyone who was engaged in the process of putting it together. I appreciate how accommodating the PPA clients have been in opening their homes—without them, these amazing projects would not have been possible. I would also like to thank the many gifted photographers, particularly Scott Frances and Jonathan Wallen, who have so compellingly brought each of them to life. Timothy Kelly's beautiful drawings, woven throughout, add another layer of interest and consistency to the book. I am most grateful to Robert A. M. Stern for providing such a sincere and gracious foreword.

A special thanks to everyone at Vendome Press, especially Mark Magowan, who has been such an enthusiastic force; Sarah Davis, whose heartfelt efforts as editor have been nothing but encouraging and helpful; and Celia Fuller, who so intuitively understood the aesthetic we desired in her graphic design. I would also like to acknowledge Tiffany Hu and Jackie Decter for their contributions.

So many people at PPA have been instrumental to bringing this book to fruition. I would like to thank Gregory Gilmartin, Anton Glikin, Elizabeth Graziolo, Mark Herring, Timothy Kelly, Pui Ng, Thomas Nugent, Nebojsa Savic, and James Malloch Taylor. Lucinda Ballard's assistance and dedication have been invaluable. I am also indebted to Aleks, George, and Marina Matviak. And finally, I would like to extend a sincere thanks to Peter Pennoyer for entrusting the work of twenty years of practice to me to write about and for turning from my coauthor to my subject with almost consistently good humor—it has been a great pleasure to work on this book and I have enjoyed every minute of it.

PAGE 1 A circular laylight illuminates the main stair of the Limestone Mansion.

PAGES 2–3 Steel French doors create a Palladian window that draws southern light into the living room of the Upper East Side Townhouse.

PAGES 4–5 The pocket doors in the dining room of the East River Apartment open onto a large gallery with fluted plaster walls.

PAGES 6–7 In the Lenox Hill Townhouse, an elliptical stair spirals up five stories under a laylight.

PAGES 8–9 The House on Penobscot Bay perches dramatically over the water.

PAGES 10–11 The library at Drumlin Hall incorporates faux bois paneling and an anthemion frieze.

PAGE 12 An upper porch at Diamond A Ranch basks in the scenery of New Mexico.

PAGE 13 A design for a house in New Jersey includes farm buildings and a guest cottage.

PAGE 12 The main stair reflects the French character of the Beaux-Arts Townhouse.

PAGES 28–29 Arched openings connect the rooms of the Fifth Avenue Triplex.

PAGES 62–63 The central stair of the Grosvenor Atterbury Townhouse runs the full height of the building.

PAGES 126–127 The porte cochere at Drumlin Hall overlooks gardens and woodlands to the west.

First published in the United States of America in 2010 by
The Vendome Press
1334 York Avenue
New York, NY 10021
www.vendomepress.com

Copyright © 2010 The Vendome Press

All rights reserved. No part of the contents of this book may be reproduced in whole or in part without prior written permission from the publisher.

ISBN 978-0-86565-268-2

EDITOR: Sarah Davis
DESIGNER: Celia Fuller

Distributed in North America by Abrams Books
Distributed outside North America by Thames & Hudson, Ltd.

Library of Congress Cataloging-in-Publication Data

Walker, Anne.
 Peter Pennoyer Architects : apartments, town houses, country houses / by Anne Walker ; foreword by Robert A.M. Stern.
  p. cm.
 ISBN 978-0-86565-268-2
 1. Peter Pennoyer Architects. 2. Architecture, Domestic--United States. 3. Classicism in architecture--United States. I. Peter Pennoyer Architects. II. Title. III. Title: Apartments, town houses, country houses.
 NA737.P393W35 2010
 728.092'2--dc22

2010015334

Printed by Toppan Printing Co., Ltd., in China
SECOND PRINTING